UNDOCUMENTED MOTHERHOOD

Louann Atkins Temple Women & Culture Series

UNDOCUMENTED MOTHERHOOD

Conversations on Love, Trauma, and Border Crossing

Elizabeth Farfán-Santos

University of Texas Press Austin

The Louann Atkins Temple Women & Culture Series is supported by Allison, Doug, Taylor, and Andy Bacon; Margaret, Lawrence, Will, John, and Annie Temple; Larry Temple; the Temple-Inland Foundation; and the National Endowment for the Humanities.

Requests for permission to reproduce material from this work should be sent to:
Permissions
University of Texas Press
P.O. Box 7819
Austin, TX 78713-7819
utpress.utexas.edu/rp-form

♾ The paper used in this book meets the minimum requirements of ANSI/NISO Z39.48-1992 (R1997) (Permanence of Paper).

Library of Congress Cataloging-in-Publication Data
Names: Farfán-Santos, Elizabeth, author.
Title: Undocumented motherhood : conversations on love, trauma, and border crossing / Elizabeth Farfán-Santos.
Other titles: Louann Atkins Temple women & culture series.
Description: First edition. | Austin : University of Texas Press, 2022. | Series: Louann Atkins Temple women & culture series | Includes bibliographical references.
Identifiers: LCCN 2022002731
ISBN 978-1-4773-2612-1 (cloth)
ISBN 978-1-4773-2613-8 (paperback)
ISBN 978-1-4773-2614-5 (PDF)
ISBN 978-1-4773-2615-2 (ePub)
Subjects: LCSH: Farfán-Santos, Elizabeth—Family. | Women noncitizens—United States—Biography. | Women noncitizens—United States—Interviews. | Women noncitizens—United States—Social conditions. | Noncitizens—Medical care—United States. | Women immigrants—United States—Social conditions. | Women immigrants—Medical care—United States. | Mexicans—United States—Social conditions. | Human smuggling—Mexican-American Border Region.
Classification: LCC JV6602 .F37 2022 | DDC 304.8/730082—dc23/eng/20220518
LC record available at https://lccn.loc.gov/2022002731

doi:10.7560/326121

Para Claudia García y todas las mamás indocumentadas
Sus vidas son mucho más que papeles.

En memoria de mi abuelita, María Luisa Farfán (1937–2020)
Para mi mamá, Elvia Farfán y
para mi hija, Anahita Farfán-Santos
Tres generaciones de mujeres finding each other anew at the
borderlands of motherhood.

CONTENTS

AUTHOR'S NOTES

A Note on Research

This book was born out of several conversations with Claudia García and my mother; however, it is also a culmination of three years of fieldwork, between 2014 and 2017, with undocumented mothers in their relationship to the public health care system in Texas and more than seven years of research on undocumented immigrant marginalization and alienation within the public health care system in the United States. Some parts of this book were introduced in lesser detail in 2019 in two scholarly papers, "The Politics of Resilience and Resistance: Health Care Access and Undocumented Mexican Motherhood in the United States" in *Latino Studies* and "Undocumented Motherhood: Gender, Maternal Identity, and the Politics of Health Care" in *Medical Anthropology: Cross-Cultural Studies in Health and Illness*. Except for my own family memories, I have changed all names and personal details.

No person in this book is complete. It was impossible to include all the hours of conversation that Claudia and I shared in this one book. Some stories just didn't fit, and others were intentionally left out, either at Claudia's request or because I felt the story revealed information that could put Claudia and her family at risk. Not everything has to be written and published. Nevertheless, there is life lived in the blank spaces between words and punctuation.

A Note on Images

The sketches throughout the book are blind contour drawings I drew of Claudia, her daughters, and her comadres using photographs. Blind contour drawings are studies. They involve drawing an image by carefully observing a subject without ever looking down at the page. I include these drawings because they are a visual representation of the broader objective of this book. The blind contour drawing requires a dedicated and intentional focus on a single subject—as did this book. In producing the drawing, the artist carefully attempts to capture the subject exactly as they are, and yet what emerges is as imperfect and complex as the subject's own story. No matter how hard and how carefully the artist observes the subject, they will never be able to fully capture them as they *truly* are. Blind contour drawings of human subjects mimic the fluid and constantly shifting reality of human life and human perspective. Every drawing, like every story, is different every time—subject and author united in perpetual motion and change.

UNDOCUMENTED MOTHERHOOD

UNDOCUMENTED MOMENTS

AFTER SEVERAL WEEKS WAITING IN TWO DIFFERENT HOST homes in the Rio Grande Valley, Claudia's coyote informed her that it was time for her daughter to leave. Nati would be traveling to Houston, Texas, without her mother, in a car with other children and a woman she had never met. "Nos dijeron que siempre estaríamos juntas," Claudia cried, "y no fue así . . . No fue así." In 2013 Claudia García and her then-two-year-old daughter, Natalia (Nati), left their small town in a region near San Luis Potosí, Mexico, to join Claudia's husband in Houston. Claudia had made the decision to cross the border because Nati was born with a hearing impairment, and she hoped that in the United States her daughter would have a chance at a better life.

I met Claudia at the Southeast Community Health Center in 2015. We met a couple of times at the clinic in the beginning, before Claudia welcomed me into her home. I remember thinking her energy was captivating. She felt young and light-spirited. Claudia was in her thirties, so she was, in fact, young, but it was more than that. Talking with her was easy from the very beginning, like we had known each other for years already. She opened up to me in a way that others didn't; she wanted me to know all of the layers of her experience, and many of those layers were wounds that were still very raw. My grandmother would've called Claudia "ligera." Claudia felt light, but I wouldn't think much about it until after I had heard her story and seen her wounds.

Through our conversations together, Claudia and I discovered that our children went to the same school. Later, they even came to share the same classroom. It wasn't a huge coincidence since the clinic where we met was in the same neighborhood as the school, and both had been part of that community for generations. When I met them, Claudia and her husband had two daughters: Nati, who was born in Mexico and takes center stage in this book, and Jackie, who was born in the United States and was just a toddler at the time. Most of our conversations took place in Claudia's living room. We'd drive over to her home after dropping our kids off at school, and there we would sit on her couch—remembering.

While Jackie napped in the other room, the early morning light still dim in the house, Claudia's most enduring memories unfolded for me over a series of episodes that, like the scenes of a captivating novela, sent me on a daily rollercoaster of emotions, awe, and disbelief. Growing up, I simultaneously loved and disliked Mexican novelas. The extreme suffering that Mexican women endure in novelas was often too much for my thirteen-year-old heart to bear. I longed for the main character to catch a break that never seemed to come soon enough—at least not until she had first been put through every trial and disaster imaginable. Every episode would ebb and flow as though resolution was just around the corner, almost there, but always just out of reach. My grandmother would laugh at my desperation and say, "La emoción es el propósito, hija. ¡El drama!" The emotion is the point, she emphasized. *Emoción* means to be saturated with feeling, passion, drama. There is purpose in emotion, in the feelings that come up in the present moment. There is suffering and struggle in the drama, but there is also passion and joy. Claudia's life story came alive for me in this way, like episodes of a novela—momentary snapshots, ongoing, still in flux. As I wrote her narrative, I was forced to give up my desire for resolution and sit with the memories and the feelings as they came up—some Claudia's and some mine.

When Claudia told me about sending Nati off with the coyote, I felt unable to find the right words. I told her I couldn't imagine how painful and frightening that must have been for her. In reality, it was more complicated than that. I couldn't help thinking of my own children. As a mother, I could imagine the terror I might feel if I had to hand my children over to strangers—

not knowing where they would go, if they would be safe, or if I would ever see them again. As a mother, I felt Claudia's tears in the pit of my stomach, un desespero that, although for me only imagined, felt thick and suffocating in its absoluteness. Sitting there with my head down, listening to her cry, I thought, My children. I could never . . . would never. . . . As a US citizen, however, I had no idea what that had *really* felt like for Claudia. Born with the privilege of "papers," I couldn't possibly know what it meant to be an undocumented mother faced with few choices, none ideal. Hand my children over to a coyote in profound hope that they would make it and have a future—or what?

I thought about my own mother, who had to send my brother and me to live in Mexico with my grandmother when we were just months old. My parents were working hard to make ends meet, but it wasn't enough. My father had just naturalized after being undocumented, and he couldn't find work. He and my mom were both teenagers; they were struggling just to buy food, and they felt they had no choice but to send us away. For Claudia, there was no alternative either. She wouldn't return to Mexico; it was not an option for her or her daughter. "Unless you have a lot of money, people like her don't make it very far over there," she said solemnly, reflecting on the additional barriers for people with disabilities in rural Mexico. Putting her daughter in the care of people she didn't know while crossing the border meant coming to terms with the reality of what would be her new life as an undocumented mother. Claudia would soon discover, however, that *undocumented* wouldn't only mean "without citizenship." It would also stand as a permanent marker of all the challenges she would have to face, and all the heartbreaking decisions she would have to make, alone. *Undocumented* would also be the physical and emotional pain that lived inside of her, and the everyday moments of joy and hope she created out of thin air—securing only small breaths for herself when possible.

I have been carrying Claudia's story—and how it relates to my story, and my mother's story—for far too long, afraid to write it for fear of getting it wrong, yet driven by the need to release it. I have felt responsible for Claudia's story, for representing it in a way that is true to the story's spirit, to its humanity and grandeur, at least as I felt it. Throughout the story's unfolding, I often found myself wandering into my own maternal history—to my mother's and grandmother's experiences. There were many instances where Claudia's stories took me back home, back to the womb. As I tell Claudia's story, mostly translated into English and forged out of the remembered episodes of her life that she chose to share with me, I weave in conversations with my own mother and grandmother. My mother's stories came up in the process of understanding Claudia's. It was impossible for me not to think back to her experiences, ones I lived and stored away in my memory but never had the courage to ask about, and others I had heard only as stories of warning. My mother's story is not the same as Claudia's; however, their narratives are connected to a type of motherhood molded by migration, the US-Mexico border, and a quest for a better future. The geopolitical border creates and shapes Mexican families on both sides; it has done so for generations. Even the very sacred notion of motherhood—what motherhood means and how it is embodied and lived by Mexican women—carries the open, throbbing, and fertile wound of the border. This book, then, is a tapestry, a weaving together of testimonios, and an intimate witnessing of motherhood between Claudia and me.

Claudia's story features a type of motherhood that often goes unnoticed, is misunderstood, and is itself undocumented—a maternal experience of love, sacrifice, and child advocacy that isn't in the parenting literature but that is nonetheless the reality of millions of (im)migrant women in the United States. While every mother has a different story, stories that recount the struggles of forming one's maternal identity through migration and displacement rarely get the attention they deserve. Societies demand everything of mothers, especially selfless sacrifice. Mothers are expected to put their children and families above everything else—their work, their personal lives, and even their own health. Mothers are supposed to sacrifice their own future for their children's future, but even *sacrifice* is political and fundamentally shaped by race, class, and political status. Immigrant mothers, especially those who migrate without formal papers, are judged very differently for their sacrifices. Fleeing across the

US-Mexico border to protect their children's lives and future is not often dignified as a selfless act of maternal love but rather charged as a selfish and criminal act—a crime punishable by state-sanctioned family separation and detention. The result is that immigrant mothers often feel compounding guilt and torment over the sacrifices they had to make during their migration. This guilt and pain, buried in their bodies, bleeds through their testimonios and sits in the silent, unspoken, unseen, and thus undocumented parts of their medical histories.

Living in the United States as an undocumented Mexican immigrant is to live with extreme uncertainty. Claudia's story, although recounted as memories, was saturated by the everyday struggles of the present moment, but also stubbornly focused on the future. In imagining and visualizing a future for her family in the US, Claudia was so focused on this vision that she felt as though if she turned away and lost focus, even for a second, even to take care of her own health, everything might fall apart forever. The moment Claudia handed her baby over to a coyote was one of the most painful of her life. It took everything out of her—the air out of her gut, the prayer from her soul. That moment, however, also spawned the rest of Nati's life in the US, and the rest of Claudia's life as an undocumented mother. Claudia sobbed through this part of her story, seemingly unable to put into words what it felt like to send her baby off without her. I didn't have the courage to ask her to explain, but my mother helped me understand. "As a mother you never forget the minute you hand your baby over to someone else . . . not sure when you will see them again," my mother said softly. "That kind of trauma, se te pega." It sticks to you.

1 | BECOMING AN UNDOCUMENTED MOTHER

"I DIDN'T WANT TO LEAVE MY HOME, MY MOTHER, MY family," Claudia recalled. "Things weren't easy in my town, but I loved it there." We were sitting together on the couch. It was still early. We had just dropped our kids off at school. Her youngest daughter, Jackie, was sleeping in the other room, and the dog was in his kennel, quiet but restless. "I lived in a small town in San Luis Potosí. My daughter Nati and I had a good life there. She was the baby, and everyone loved her a lot and protected her. Recently I had discovered that Nati was sick in her ears. I told [my husband] and that's why he told us to leave. He told me there were more opportunities to help her over here in the United States. 'Arregla tus cosas y te vienes,' he said. In reality, I didn't have a choice, but I learned to understand he was right. Entonces nos venimos. I left on October 17 or 19 of 2013. We left that day for real."

As Claudia spoke, I thought back to the day I left for real. There aren't many things I remember about my childhood, but I do remember the time my brother and I went to live with my grandmother in San Luis Potosí. I remember that we went without my parents, but I didn't know then that my parents had to stay back in Houston to work, to make money to support our family. My mom was born in Chicago. Like many Mexican immigrants, her parents migrated from Monterrey to Pilsen on the Lower West Side of Chicago in the 1940s, and that's where she lived until she met my dad, a young immigrant from San Luis

Potosí who happened to show up at my grandfather's taqueria, where my mom was a waitress. Undocumented and struggling to find work, my dad had only been living in the United States for a couple of years. He wasn't even in his twenties, but he was already responsible for his mother and siblings. Just a few years after meeting my father, my mom would agree to leave everything she knew in the US and move to Mexico to try to build a life for her growing family—or maybe just because she couldn't stand being away from us. It doesn't really matter. I like the idea of both.

"Mi experiencia de migrarnos fue horrible, muy feo." Claudia accentuated "muuuy feo," shaking her head slowly from side to side as though still in disbelief of her own experience, her own story. "We came with a coyote. I was with my daughter, and all I knew was that we would be delivered to my husband in Houston, Texas. My stepfather took us to the border and left us there with a man. He was short and impatient. I'm not sure why I remember he was short. Maybe it was just my nerves trying to distract me. We had to say our goodbyes quickly. You can't stand around, you know, and say ni ya me voy, ni ya vine. They just told us to get in a van and we left. The ride was quiet. My husband had organized everything, so I had no idea where they were taking me. When the van stopped, we were dropped off at a house where we stayed until we could successfully cross the river. I didn't know who lived there, but there were a lot of men there—yes, mostly men.

"I crossed the river by boat. They didn't want us to get anything wet, not even our feet, so when we got closer to land, they took us and carried us the rest of the way. But then all of a sudden someone would yell, '¡La migra! La migra is coming!' And we had to all go back to the boat again, and we couldn't cross until we knew it was safe. We would go back and forth like that again and again, or we'd go back to the house and wait another day. The day we finally crossed into El Valle, it took two attempts. We tried at 9 a.m. and then again at four in the afternoon. That time it was quick. That's when we went to El Valle to stay with a family. There were two little girls, the mom, and the man that brought me. My daughter and I stayed there for fifteen days. They treated us very well there, but every day I would ask, 'When are we leaving? When are we leaving?' I couldn't wait to get out of there—to be safe with my husband. They treated us well there, but who knew how long that would last. I was still very nervous not knowing what the plan was or when it would all be over, and they wouldn't tell me anything. I would only find out about a part of the plan when it was happening."

Claudia took a deep breath, then continued. "Me dijeron que le comprara un medicamento a la niña para que se durmiera. Pero me decían que poquito, verdad, para que se durmiera y no hiciera ruido. En ese momento yo sentí mucho, mucho miedo. ¿Qué tal si me pasaba de medicamento y se podía hasta morir, verdad? Ella tenía apenas dos añitos y no sabía nada de lo que estaba pasando, y yo le decía, 'Cállate,' pero ella no me entendía. Me duele mucho recordar esa experiencia. I think now about everything that could have happened, how it could have ended differently." Claudia paused, surrendering to the tears. I could tell that it was very painful for her to recall some of the decisions she was forced to make during her migration, especially when it came to her daughter. Leaving this part of her story untranslated preserves some of the intimacy of the moment.

Our conversation was briefly interrupted by the garbage truck. It came barreling down the street, letting us all know it was coming. "¡Híjole! Hold on a minute. I forgot to put the trash out." Claudia got up and ran through the house picking up trash cans from the bathroom, bedrooms, and kitchen. "Do you need help?" I asked. "¿Como crees? No, disculpa. ¡Solo un minutito!" She apologized over and over for the interruption as she tried to catch up with the truck, the dog going wild as he watched her run back and forth. When she came back in, she was laughing and trying to catch her breath. "You should've seen me running after that truck! ¡Como una loca!" Claudia's spirit had changed in those two minutes of chasing the garbage truck. She had ánimo again and even seemed cheerful. It reminded me that I had invaded her privacy. I was invited into her home to record her story, yes, but it was an invasion nonetheless. It was the only place where she could put away the smile and feel whatever she needed to feel. Her home. Her sanctuary. And there I was, asking her to open old wounds.

"Okay, where were we?" She started again. Back to remembering. "They took us to another house. I tried to see where we were going, to see an address or something because one never knows, but I couldn't. In that house there were three women and many men, then another woman arrived. We were still on the border, I knew that. From there they took us to another house, and from there to another house, and then they would take me to where the truck was. That's where they prepared me for the trip. And that's when I had to leave her. I left, and she had to stay. I begged them to let me take her. 'How is she going to stay? Why?' I cried. 'How will she cross? Who will take her? Why do you leave her, and why can't I bring her with me?' They had told me that she would be with me the entire time, but it wasn't like that. She was not with me the entire time, but I couldn't do anything about it. I had to leave her. Y me fui bien preocupada. En mi mente yo decía, '¿Y la niña? ¿Y la niña?' Sometimes even I think it was all just a nightmare. But when I saw how I would cross, I was glad Nati wasn't with me. I couldn't believe it. You know the top part of the trucks? There's like a hood at the top, a hole at the very top. That's where they put me."

Later, when I got back to my office, I looked into it and found out Claudia was talking about the roof fairing. According to the Society of Automobile Engineers (SAE) website, a roof fairing is a truck add-on that "reduces the aerodynamic drag on the vehicle." There are different types and sizes, but the one Claudia was referring to was large and, in the language of the SAE, "highly curved and bulbous," the best for "reducing drag" and improving fuel efficiency. Claudia would travel to Texas in the roof fairing of an eighteen-wheeler truck. Scanning through pictures of different trucks and roof fairings, I knew from past research that many immigrants had traveled inside roof fairings and other parts of large trucks across the border. I remembered one news report about how Immigration stopped a truck on the border and found migrants stuffed inside spare tires, and another report of dozens of migrants being found dead after the truck they were traveling in exploded. It appeared that people had been shoved inside an empty gas tank. My thoughts wandered to what an SAE meeting would look like if these engineers knew this and decided to include it on their website. I wondered, What would be the aerodynamic drag and the added fuel cost of two migrant bodies?

"They pushed my body into that hole," Claudia continued, "along with another man, and right there, I learned that two people fit in there. I never would have known, but I know now. The truck was already turned on, and the hot metal burned my skin, but I had to stay quiet because the truck driver had no idea we were there. They had just chosen any truck that had Texas plates. That's all they cared about was that it was going to Texas. Shoved into that truck, I understood why Nati couldn't come with me, and I thanked God for keeping her away. They gave us a phone with a GPS that they would use to track us until we arrived. And so, we left. Well, we were on our way, and then the coyote sent us a message saying we just had ten more minutes left and we'd be across. Then all of a sudden, the truck stops, and the doors sound off, and we hear, '¡Oye, tú! Bájate!' We got so scared, so we both came out. 'What do you think you're doing?' the truck driver yelled. 'Who put you in there? You can't do that! ¡No se puede!' We explained that they told us to get in the roof of the truck, and he got really angry. '¡No! Bájense! You can get me in so much trouble.' And me, I was crying, begging him for the love of God. 'We won't make any noise! We won't make any noise. Please let us on. Please take us with you just until we pass.'

"'Do you understand that I can go to jail or worse? I don't even know! No! I'm not taking you anywhere.' He left us there, in the desert, and all we could do was run to find somewhere to hide. I called my husband crying, hysterical. I said, 'Papi, he threw us off the truck!' 'But how?' he asked. 'Let me talk to the driver. He knows!' 'I'm telling you he doesn't know anything. He's the one that threw us off,' I cried.

"Well, night came and there we were, this man and me in the desert alone. I called the coyote that put us in the truck, and he told us to wait for him to come get us. He told us, 'When I get there, I will honk twice, then you come out and get in the car.' He took a while to get there. When he finally arrived, he honked once, and well, I was so scared, I ran out, but he wouldn't let me in the car. Then he honked the second time, and the man ran out. He yelled, 'I was already going to leave you both here because there's a lot of Immigration out here! And you, Mexicana'—they called me Mexicana—'I told you the second honk! I told you to wait until the second honk! I was going to leave you there!' They really put the fear of God in you because they're so mean, te hablan bien feo. They yell at you and tell you all kinds of things to scare you, that they'll leave you to die if you don't listen. Es muy feo.

"They put us in another truck, and then the same thing happened. The driver threw us off and left us again. This time the coyote had stayed close by and picked us up faster. It was a good thing too because it was even later in the night. It was around 3 a.m. Even though it was late, we would have to keep trying. The coyote drove us to a gas station and told us to run and get in any truck that had Texas plates. '¡Súbanse a cualquier camión prendido! Nada más fíjense que diga Tejas.' And we were like, 'No, no, and no!'

"The truck drivers were already staring at us, probably wondering what we were up to. But I didn't have a choice. I walked around holding this man's hand, hugging him, pretending to be his girlfriend or wife or something. Trying to act natural, I guess. We ran around hiding behind the wheels of trucks looking for Texas plates, but there weren't many, and none of them were turned on. I got scared and said I wouldn't do it anymore, that I wouldn't get on any truck! The coyote yelled at me so bad. He threatened me that if I didn't find a truck and get on, they would leave me there so that some other gang would get me, and that they would probably cut out my eyes or kill me! They really put the fear of God into you."

"And where was your little girl this whole time?" I asked, briefly interrupting.

"With them!" Claudia said. "She was with them! So that terrified me even more, right? Because I knew they had my daughter. I called my husband, desperate, crying, to tell him they wanted to leave me behind. He called the original coyote that took me across the river, because supposedly he was the one responsible for me, and he told him I didn't want to go like that anymore. I guess it worked because the next thing I knew they had sent some other men to get me and take me back to the house. When I got there, it was late. I found my little girl sleeping on the floor. Someone had laid out a single sheet for her to lie on. It made me sad to see her there on the floor because at that time it was already starting to get cold, but what could I do? I laid down next to her, held her close, and just tried to sleep."

Thirty-two years before Claudia left Mexico, my mother made her own decision to leave the United States. When I asked if I could interview her about her migration story, she smiled nervously, trying not to make eye contact, and said, "Pos si, okay," reluctantly adding, "Right now?" "Yeah, right now, if that's okay," I responded, also trying to avoid eye contact. "Okay. Um . . . Okay." She shuffled some papers off the table, smoothed the surface, and sat down. My daughter, then just months old, was running around, throwing things on the floor. My grandmother was in the kitchen washing the dishes, just listening. I meant to talk with her afterward, but I wouldn't get the chance.

I guess I was nervous to talk with my mom because I knew I would uncover old wounds, hers and mine, just as I had done with Claudia. Maybe I should call myself a wound-poker instead of an anthropologist. Either way, there we were. Claudia's migration story, especially the heartbreaking parts where she was separated from her daughter, got me thinking about what my mom might have felt when she was separated from us. I remember our time in Mexico fondly, like an adventure I sometimes thought I had dreamt up. It was forever stamped in my memory as "The Time I Lived With My Grandmother," in title caps, like the chapter of a book. But it wasn't until I heard Claudia cry as she recalled all the times she had to leave Nati and thought about all the things that could have happened that I really stopped to think about what that time must have been like for my mom— what she must have felt during those years.

"I was going, and they were coming," my mom remembered, looking down and shaking her head. "All these people are coming here to the United States, and I was going to Mexico to be with you guys. It's not easy over there, you know, trying to make a life with pesos. It was so hard. I left Chicago in 1981, or end of '81, I think. There was no work there for us, and we needed money. We had just gotten married, and your brother was less than a year old. My sister told us there was a lot of work in Texas, and your dad couldn't find work in Chicago. Your dad was trying to find a truck driving job, and I was trying to find a job too because his didn't make very much, and we didn't have enough money. We had to send your grandma money in Mexico, and your dad was trying to make ends meet for everyone. When we moved to Texas, we stayed with my sister in Galena Park, but she was getting mad because we weren't paying for groceries. So when your dad got a job, with his first paycheck we tried to get an apartment. Then we were saving, and with the second paycheck we gave her money for groceries. That's when your grandma said, 'Why don't you bring him over here, so you can work?'

"Humberto went first. I think he stayed maybe two months, but I couldn't take it, and I wanted to go get him again. So we brought him back, and then that's when your grandma came to the States. By that time, we had an apartment. I think it was maybe six months later. Your grandma stayed a while and then went back. When I got pregnant with you a few months after she left, she came back to help me with the pregnancy. Our apartment was in Pasadena at that time, and we were having trouble paying the rent because I had you and I had to stop working. I think you were like a month old or six weeks when your grandma again said, because it was hard, because it was your grandma and your uncle, I don't remember who was all here, but there were like two other people staying here with us, and . . ."

I could tell my mom was hesitating. Explaining as much as she could, trying to make sure I understood the context, the reason why she did what she did, before continuing. It was like she was trying to soften the blow even though I already knew what came next. She paused, then went on. "Your grandma said, 'Why don't I take her and Beto back with me so that you can work?' And I said yes, because . . . what could I say? It was really hard. Day care was so expensive, and there was no way we could afford it. But again, it was too much for me, and after a while, I don't remember exactly, I had to go get you guys. I was working, but I was sad all the time. I cried every day. I couldn't last without you guys, so I left. I went to Mexico to be with you. While I was there, your dad called me and said, 'Why don't we try to make a life in Mexico?' I didn't see another way. I couldn't leave you guys again, but we also couldn't afford to live in the States. So I said okay. What other choice did I have?"

I couldn't help thinking about my dad and Claudia's husband. They had both proposed the idea of moving their families across the border in hopes of making it. Neither Claudia nor my mother were excited about leaving behind everything they knew and loved. "I didn't have a choice, but I learned to understand he was right," Claudia had recalled. "I didn't see another way," my mom said. For them, migration wasn't really a choice. No one was forcing them, but everything was forcing them. It was bigger than them. It was about their children, their families, survival, faith, and the possibility of a better future. Their own needs would have to wait.

"At that time your grandma had bought a food truck," my mom went on. "It wasn't a mobile truck. It was more like a cart. So I said okay, I'll stay and help her sell food, and we tried that for a while until we decided to open a little grocery store. Your dad stayed in the States for about a year, or maybe less, and then finally came back too. I think it was when Hurricane Alicia hit. That's when Dad left. He took some of our furniture and came to be with us in Mexico. We were running the store and trying to sell food when something happened with the food truck. In the food truck we would sell tacos, arroz, frijoles, carne, plates of food. Me and Grandma made all of it. We used to wake up like at 6 a.m. to go to the market and get all the things we needed. Then we'd cook all day and sell it the next day. It was a lot of work.

"I remember these señoras would come talk to me in the market. They acted so nice. I told them I was from Chicago and that I had just moved to San Luis. Then, can you believe? I found out they were going around telling people, 'Mira esa se cree que es de Chicago. ¡Te apuesto que es del mercadito!' My mom burst into laughter, remembering how people thought she was lying about being from Chicago—that she was just trying to show off. 'In their minds who was going to leave the States to sell tacos in the market?' she chuckled.

"One day your dad was making shelves for the store, and he cut his leg. After that happened, we had to spend a lot of money in the hospital. His leg kept getting infected, so we had to go to specialists, which also cost a lot of money. After the food truck stopped working, we had decided to focus on the store. But when your dad cut his leg, we couldn't afford the store either. Because all of our money was going to pay for your dad's treatments, we couldn't afford to stock the store anymore, and finally we said, 'This is too much.' So that's when I had to go out to the street markets and sell. Can you imagine that? Me standing in the middle of a market yelling? You know I don't like attention like that. But I did it. I watched how the women yelled and called out, and I just copied them. '¡Ándele, dígame que va a llevar, señora! Dígame, ¿cuál va a llevar?' I called out. Your grandma thought it was so funny. She would just laugh watching me. And then, well, I did become 'del mercadito,'" my mom laughed.

"There were seven of your tías and tíos, and your grandpa and grandma, and us and everyone had been living off the store. So the money was getting less and less because nobody was working. Your tías were all in school, so money was going out the window, and then your dad decides to cut his leg! So our situation got even worse. Money was going out the window, and no money was coming in, so it was hard. When I was with you guys, I was working the store, and we were always working, so we never had any time for fun activities. We didn't go to the park. We didn't go anywhere fun. Everything was just work, work, work. When Dad cut his leg, he said, 'You know what? We're not doing this anymore.' And when he got better, he said, 'I'm going back to the States.' But what happened was he didn't have any money to come back. His leg was getting better. It took a long time, and he had to get therapy and couldn't walk for months, but thank God, it got better. We had to buy this real expensive medicine to cure the infection, because the infection was spreading, and either we bought the medicine, or he could lose his leg. We put all of our money into making sure he got better!

When he got better, he was trying to find work, but nobody would hire him. One day he went out to look for work because we were at the point that we couldn't even buy food to eat. Dad took your grandpa's motorcycle. He had his sister on the back, and they crashed. A gas truck went in front of them and threw them off the road. It was my birthday, and he didn't have any money to even buy me a flower.

"When Dad finally got back to the States, your godfather found him a job right away. That was the good thing! It took him a few weeks, and then he started sending us money again. We had to stay in Mexico because we didn't have any money to go back with him. But as soon as we had enough money, I said, 'I'm going back home.' I got you guys and said, 'Let's go home.'"

My mom added emphasis when she remembered her decision to "go back home." Her intonation made it clear that what she remembered the most was that she was determined to leave Mexico and make it at home, in the States. At that time she only had enough money for our bus tickets, so she knew it was a gamble and that the struggle wouldn't be over. I see now that she made that decision because it was what she needed to do. Claudia made a similar gamble for herself when she stood up to the coyote and refused to get on another truck.

"The next day, the first thing I did was tell them I wouldn't go on any more trucks! '¡Prefiero irme a pie!' I'd rather walk." Claudia shook her head as she recalled the moment she stood up to the coyote. She remembered being terrified of what would happen next and how she ended up sorely regretting her words "Prefiero irme a pie."

"They agreed to take us back to the coyote that was responsible for me, back in El Valle, so that's what we did. Nati and I stayed with him for maybe two or three days until he finally said, 'Get ready because today, you will leave.' I was so relieved. It was the same as the last time. I got ready and again I said goodbye to my daughter, and I left. I didn't know anything. I knew I would go walking, that was all. The coyote put us in the back of a small truck. There were seven of us, and the driver was some woman. Well, this woman decided that with all of us in the truck, it was a good idea to stop at a gas station. And that's where it happened. As we were walking out of the gas station, ¡pún! We get stopped by Immigration.

"I think that was the most horrifying moment of my life. They didn't even ask us anything. They just took all of us and locked us up. I spent five days locked up in a detention center. I just remember I cried, and I cried, '¡Mi niña, mi niña!' They wouldn't let me use the phone, so I couldn't even call anyone to tell them where I was. I was so desperate and scared. I couldn't call my husband or my daughter! It was horrible, just horrible. They don't let you sleep at all in there, not even for a minute. Bueno, I never slept. It's like a hielera in there. ¡Friísimo! It was so cold, and they don't give you a blanket or anything. I had a sweater with me, but they took it. They took all my things.

"It was like being in a jail, but it was a detention center, a detention center in Mission, Texas, that's where it was. Y la comida era horrible. The food was horrible. Twice a day, every day, they fed us a sandwich of plain white bread and Spam, no mayonnaise or anything, and a small juice box, nothing else. It was disgusting. The bathroom was also just for show—a short wall with no door, open for all to see. The camera was there too, always watching. I don't know if it actually recorded us, but it didn't matter anyway because everyone else could see you. I tried really hard not to use the bathroom. There were at least eighty women in one tiny room. We had to try to sleep sitting up because we didn't all fit. They separated all of us, the women in one place, the men in another, and the children in another.

"There came a day when they finally called me. They put me in front of a camera and took my picture, my fingerprints, they asked me my name, if I had tattoos, and where I lived. From there they sent me to another agent where they forced me to sign a deportation for five years. I had no choice but to sign the deportation. I signed it, and they returned me to my cell. When the time came for me to be deported, the bus came for me and some others. They just threw us in and threw us out. They pushed us out of the bus, uncuffed us, because they handcuff you, and threw us in Reynosa. They told us to walk across the bridge to get to the other side, but before you get across, they stop you at the bridge and take your picture again and tell you to sign another paper. When I got back to Mexico, I had nothing. They took everything from me at the detention center. I had nothing left. So you find yourself in the streets of a city you don't know, with nothing in your possession, and all you can think of is where do I go now? What do I do?

"Everyone took off in their own direction, but I stuck with a woman. I didn't want to separate from her. I wanted to call my husband, of course! Because in those five days I hadn't had contact with anyone. As soon as I found a phone, I called my husband. I told him everything that happened. He had been so worried. He asked me if I was okay and if I needed money. I didn't because I still had money he had given me. When I got off the phone with him, I started to walk over to a nearby bank, but I noticed there were two guys following us. I overheard one of them on the phone saying they were going to rob us. The woman and I slipped into an Elektra store and waited them out. We walked around pretending like we actually belonged there, like we were going to buy something.

"After a long time, we left and ran over to a plaza. There we were picked up by the coyote. He took us to another house. It didn't look like a house anyone actually lived in though. It was burned all over and falling apart. It was horrifying. The only person in the house was an elderly woman. But even though the house looked scary on the outside, they treated us so well there. They treated us like people, como gente. There they fed us well and gave us decent food and drink! I was a little stick— skinny, skinny—from all those days in detention that I didn't eat. I couldn't eat. I was so stressed with worry over my daughter. I had no communication with her! I had left her in that house, but I didn't know if she was safe or if she was even still there. How could I know? I didn't have contact with anyone!

"Well, we knew we were going to try to cross over again, but this time it took us two days. I thought it would be the same as the last time. I mean, it was the same river, but this time it was different. The part of the river where we would cross was wider and deeper. It felt enormous! We crossed in a metal boat with a lot of other people, and all I could think was, What if I fall out? I can't swim! I'll die! I remember the coyotes gave everyone nick-names. They told me, when you get across, tell them you're with Azul. It was some man they called El Azul. They warned us not to say anything else. 'Don't tell them you came from Michoacán or San Luis or anything. Just say you came with this guy or that guy,' they said. My guy was El Azul.''

"We came on the bus. I didn't want to stay anymore. It was just too much. We worked too hard and couldn't make enough money. It was nice being there because we were with family, y sea como sea, that helps a lot, but it's hard to live. If you don't have a professional job, it's impossible to live. To just be a street vendor and work, with no education, it's very hard to live. Very, very hard. I was eighteen. I was very young and very inexperi-enced. I had a hard time finding work because my education wasn't, um . . . wasn't very high. I didn't finish high school, so when we went back to the States, and eventually your grandma came too, I took advantage of that and went to get my diploma so I could at least have that."

My mom wasn't a big talker, and this conversation with me was difficult for her. I never knew my mom to share her feel-ings with us. In fact, she once told us that "those were not con-versations that should be had with kids." "Children should not be burdened with their parents' problems," she counseled. My father agreed. I sensed my mom had finished or was finishing her story, so I pushed her a little to talk about her feelings. "What did it feel like for you, living over there all those years?" I asked cautiously. She took a deep breath, turned her gaze back down, and twisted her hands together on the table.

"You were almost two, and your brother was almost four. Your brother was in kindergarten, and you were a baby. It was good because I had a lot of help! Yous had a lot of aunts, and Grandma and Grandpa always carried you. Everyone was always taking care of you. It was good and bad because everyone took care of you, but I would just see you at night because I was working all day in the store. You had all your tías to take care of you. That was good. But I was sad. I felt like I missed out on a lot of your lives because I was working. Sometimes I would cry."

She stopped, overwhelmed by her tears. "Don't cry, Mom," I said softly with a knot in my throat. This part was hard to sit through and hard again to transcribe. We were both crying, but the television in the background held the silence away, muffling our tears on the recording. My daughter was still running around the room, getting into things she wasn't supposed to. My grandmother was quietly observing from the kitchen. My mom stared at her hands, rubbing them intensely, trying to stop the tears. She didn't cry often, and I could tell she was holding in a lot of pain. The pain of everything she did and didn't do, of lost moments, of time that passed too fast. "Can you tell me why you're crying?" I asked, in part because I didn't know what else to say. She tried to respond, pausing to cry every few words.

"Because sometimes I think, I, um . . . I know Dad wanted to help his family, and I did too. But sometimes I think I . . . I affected my own family a lot along the way. But I guess for being such a young person, I was . . . I was very responsible. But my kids. My kids. I was working too much and not giving my kids enough time, which . . . you guys were very happy because you got to be around a lot of family, and you had a lot of love because everyone loved you so much. It's not like you needed love because you had it. But I feel like I . . . I wanted . . . to give you . . . more time. But I feel like . . . we could've done more for *my* family, for us, and not tried to do so much for everyone else. Because it was just too many of us, and trying to live on pesos was . . . very hard. But I think that either way, God was good to us. You were both healthy. You never got sick. Your brother never got sick. A lot of times, you would eat dirt! Suck on rocks! But you were healthy." She laughed and cried thinking about how illness spared us.

"I think you had a real nice childhood because you had so much love. Everyone was so nice to both you and your brother. It was sad because it was a lot of work, just work, and then when your dad came back to the States, it was just me, and that was even harder. I was so busy sometimes that I wouldn't have time to think of the sadness, but when I would go to my room at night to relax, I would get sad because we never did anything together. We just worked. Sometimes when I got really sad about everything, the only thing that made me happy was I had one album of Michael Jackson that I would play in my room, and that would make me happy. It would remind me of home."

"They told me it was time for her to leave." Claudia had suddenly slowed down in her story. Her voice grew softer, almost faint. "She would go in a car with a woman and other children. They gave me five minutes to get her ready and say goodbye. I put milk, food, and some extra clothes in her backpack, all of the little things she might need. I blessed her, put her in her car seat, and, well, said goodbye." Claudia paused, overwhelmed by tears. She put one hand over her face, tightly squeezing her eyes as if she were trying to slow the agony of each tear. "I mean I said goodbye but tried to explain to her that I would see her again soon. It was horrible. It was the hardest thing I've ever done in my life, even with everything that had already happened to me. I wasn't ready for this, but what else could I do but pray that God protect her for me, that God guide her path and take care of her where I couldn't?

"It felt like an eternity, but maybe an hour later they called me to tell me she had crossed safely. I was so relieved because I thought she was with her dad. She was safe. But then they told me that she wouldn't be given to her dad until I arrived. The deal was that we both had to be turned in together, and that's what they would do. They told me that only when I arrived would they turn her in. They would turn us in together. They took her to a house. I had no idea where she was. I begged them, for the love of God, to take her to her dad, but they wouldn't listen. What could I do? I spent fifteen days, fifteen days without seeing my daughter—not even knowing where she was.

"En eso, they told me to get ready because it was time for me to leave too. I changed my clothes, put on my tennis shoes and jeans. I put on two pairs of pants and two shirts, and I tied my things inside of my clothes. I tied my cell phone around my chest and turned it off because they wanted everything turned off, because if an airplane or helicopter flies over us, then that's how they can detect us. They put us in a car and drove us to the trailer that would take us across. They put me in the front end of the trailer because I was wearing a fluorescent-colored shirt, and who would've thought I would be trying to cross illegally wearing that, right? Everyone else was in the back, crouched down and hidden. Some people went in the trunk. Imagine that! Can you imagine that? There were a hundred and thirty people in that trailer—people from Honduras, Guatemala, and different parts of Mexico. They separated us into groups, each group in different parts of the trailer. Everyone was carefully organized because there was a lot of Immigration in that area. At night we had to keep all the lights off. It was so dark.

"I've never experienced that kind of darkness. I couldn't see anything, not even my own hands, but I could hear everything. I was there trying not to let my fear take over when I heard a woman. I couldn't tell at first if they grabbed her or she went on her own because all I heard was that a man called her outside and she went, but there were other men out there waiting for her. I heard them rape her. I heard her scream. I heard her beg, que no quería, that she didn't want to. She cried, but it was too late, and there were too many of them. They covered her mouth. Her screams were muffled, but we could all still hear all of it. It was horrifying. Everyone was too scared, I think, to do anything to help her. Me and some of the other women started to cry. I think we were all thinking the same thing. We were all waiting for them to come back and rape all of us. We didn't have any protection. We couldn't stop it if it happened. We were outnumbered. I don't know how long it was, but eventually the woman came back in the trailer crying. I wasn't raped that night. It was just luck or God, or I don't know. I spent three days in that trailer. Like that.

"When they finally came to get us, they separated us into groups of thirty. They gave us each a gallon of water, and they took us into the woods and made us wait until around seven at night before we started walking. We walked and walked. And all of a sudden someone would yell 'Run! Run!' and we would all run and find a bush to hide behind. They had these plastic capes that we used to cover ourselves so we would blend in with the bushes. They would tell us to close our hands into fists because our nails shone white in the night. The same thing with our eyes.

We had to keep them closed so the whites of our eyes didn't shine in the night just like cat eyes. We had walked for hours, for eight hours, I think. I was so tired, I couldn't handle anymore. No aguantaba los pies. I couldn't stand the pain in my feet. I was ready to give up and, well . . . die there in the desert, but there was a man that pulled me up and dragged me along. 'Ándale, Mexicana, camina,' he said. 'You can't die here.' We rested for a few minutes and then we kept going, but I couldn't stand my feet. They were covered in blisters and bleeding. It was horrible. Along the path we walked over cadavers. The whole time we could hear the howling of wolves. We came across snakes. They kept telling us to stay together. We couldn't lose each other or else we wouldn't make it alone out there.

"When we finally arrived, we came to a big highway. I know now it's called a freeway. Well, we had to cross it, and I couldn't do it. I didn't have the strength to run that entire distance. I cried and resigned myself to give up. I was going to stay there because I couldn't go any further. But the man that was helping me grabbed me again and dragged me across. It took everything I had to push myself through that last stretch. I thought to myself, Just one last run and then I'll be there. I thought about seeing my daughter and how I didn't know if she was safe or where she was, and how she wouldn't be safe until I was with her. I had to use all the power I had to get my body across that freeway.

"When we all got across, they put us in the back of a truck, packed us into rows like sardines, some looking forward and others looking back, like that, and the women all in front. I have no idea how we all fit because there were thirty of us! We traveled another two hours in that truck until we got to Houston. We were all dirty and exhausted. Our pants were covered in stickers. You know those things that stick to your clothes? There were so many stickers all over my body, ¡pero muchos! Tuvimos que aguantar así un buen rato.

"In Houston we came to another house. They got us in quickly and separated us into different rooms. I think they treated us women much better than the men. Yes, there they did. They took all the men to other rooms and locked them in with a key.

Us, they gave us all our own little bed and let us take a shower. There they sold clothes in case we wanted to change. When it was my time to leave the house, it got a little complicated for me because my husband didn't answer the phone, and the coyote in charge of me didn't answer either. Nobody was answering my calls. I was scared and confused.

"They prepared me for the pickup. They told me that I couldn't get too excited. No hugs, no kisses, nothing. Someone could be watching us, and that kind of emotion could give us away, and then we could be followed. Can you imagine how hard that was for me? When I got in the car and saw my husband, all I wanted to do was hug him. I hadn't seen him in two years! Two years! And after everything I had just been through, I just wanted to hug him, but he just squeezed my knee and said, 'Ya, ya estás aquí.' I opened my mouth to ask, but before I could say anything, he said, 'We're on our way to see her.' I was relieved to see my husband, but I was still concerned about my daughter. Yo estaba al pendiente de la niña. En ese momento no sabía nada. He told me she was with his family at my sister-in-law's home. On our way there he explained to me that he had picked her up at a different gas station earlier. That's why he didn't answer my calls. She wasn't well. Estaba mal. She was all dirty and had a terrible rash. She was in so much pain, they had to take her diaper off because it hurt her so much. Her skin was all red and swollen. I just cried listening to him.

"When we got to my sister-in law's home, my husband wanted me to talk to everyone. He showed me off with pride and wanted to introduce me to all his sisters, but I only cared about my daughter. I apologized to everyone because the first thing I said was 'Where is my daughter?' Can you believe that the same day I arrived, someone had broken into my sister-in-law's house to rob them? Everything was thrown around and broken. It was terrifying to see, and all I could do was go to my daughter as fast as possible. She was in the back room asleep. I ran and picked her up, and I hugged her so tight. She said, '¿Ma? ¿Mamá?' At that time that's all she could say. In that moment, I did cry. I cried so much out of relief and happiness to see her, to be there with her, and to know that we were safe. She showed me her little donkey and all her toys that her dad had bought her. I told you, mi historia migratoria es muy fea, muy, muy fea."

I wonder what Nati will remember from her migration. Will she remember leaving her mom, just as Claudia remembers leaving hers? Will she remember the border and the different houses? Will she remember it as an adventure or as trauma? Will she remember how loved she was in Mexico and then in the United States? Both Claudia and my mom emphasize the love and support of family throughout their migrations. Despite the struggles and difficult moments, there were many moments of love and protection. Even though she understood that Nati's future was uncertain in Mexico, Claudia felt loved and protected there. She had a family that loved her and her daughter, and a home that was good and safe. Even though my mom felt sad and overwhelmed in Mexico, she knew her children were loved and protected there, and that was reason enough to keep trying. Claudia still dreams of one day returning to Mexico. The struggle, sacrifice, and trauma had not erased the moments of love and joy. It's contradictory, perhaps, but they exist simultaneously.

They say that what remains in our memories, especially our earliest childhood memories, is more how we felt and not so much the details of what happened. Or, perhaps, emotions magnify the details that our body chooses to remember.[1] Trauma research on migrant children has shown that they can exhibit trauma from migration even if they were very young when they migrated.[2] But lives are complex, and I like to think that Nati will remember different stories about her migration. The truth is that Claudia will likely come up with a number of different versions of Nati's migration—a version for Nati, a version for herself, and versions she chooses to share with others. All will be real and valid because all are rooted in Claudia's experiences, and each story will be born out of all the layers of her life in any given moment.

For years, my mother's version of her migration, the story she told me and that was recounted in family gatherings, didn't include her at all. The stories I heard were always about how

much my grandmother and aunts cared for me; these were specific memories recounted in great detail, down to the sounds
and smells, with joy and care always the focus. It wasn't until
many years later that I asked for the bigger story and forced my
mother to include herself, her memories, and her wounds in
the narrative. It was only then that I saw a different side of her
experience. The same is true for Claudia and Nati. Their memories are just as alive and in flux as they are, and their stories will
morph and flow with their relationship and needs at different
moments in their lives.

I like to think that Nati will also remember feeling loved and
protected. That she will know that her grandparents, tíos, and tías
loved her so much they gave every dollar they could to help her
cross the border so that she might have the chance for a better
life. I like to think that Nati's memory will include how her
mother walked across the world, over snakes and cadavers, just
for her.

"Nobody dreams of becoming an undocumented mother,"
Claudia would later tell me. She had faced the border—and all
of its horrors—and survived. She will tell you that it was "God
or luck" that she made it; even she can't believe it sometimes. I
know that Nati will remember her migration, and I think it will
be a title-case chapter in her life too, but only time will tell what
that chapter will look like for her and how it will influence her
life. As a mother, however, I worry about Claudia too. Mothers
don't always get compassion and time to grieve their losses and
traumas. Sometimes they are the dam holding back the raging
waters so that their children can run free, and they do, even if
just for a moment. But what happens to the mother, her back
bruised and swollen from the raging waters?

Becoming undocumented added another level of burden and
erasure to Claudia's maternal experience. Everything she experienced on the border would forever be a part of her memory
of Nati's childhood, but it wouldn't get a special photo album or
memory book. Claudia would likely skip over it when people
asked about Nati's toddler years, highlighting instead the lovely
experiences she had in Mexico and then seamlessly transitioning
to her new life in Houston. The family would come up with

jokes molded out of the cutest and silliest memories—"Remember when Nati used to crawl behind the couch and scared us because we couldn't find her!"—and just like that, the joy of the memory of Nati crawling around her home in Mexico would take over the conversation in sweet nostalgia. The migration—the in-between, the how we got here, an unspoken presence—was a story Claudia would carry inside of her that might only come out again if Nati decided to ask about it one day.

Claudia and her daughter survived the border. So many women and children don't. Sitting on that couch with Claudia in her home, which she created, while Nati started her day at school and Jackie slept safely in her bed, I found it hard to believe that this encounter might have never happened if things had gone differently. Claudia is still tormented by the most painful details of her migration, the ones she told me and the ones she didn't. She shared that she still had nightmares, and still found herself suddenly sad and crying "así de la nada," out of nowhere. Later I would understand more clearly what she meant, and just how deeply the scars of the border were forever marked on her body.

2 | FALSAS ESPERANZAS

"I FOUND OUT WHEN SHE WAS AROUND ONE THAT SHE was malita. My husband didn't have health insurance from his job, so he had to apply for one on his own. It was really complicated because he doesn't have a Social Security number, so at first they told him he couldn't buy it, that it was too much paperwork, too complicated, but after a lot of fighting and, well, begging and begging, they finally gave it to us. We paid eight hundred dollars a month. It was a lot, but we needed a good insurance that would cover her specialists.

"At first, I just took her to the community clinic down the street, but from there they sent us to the Speech Center. I took her there for therapy for a whole year because we knew she would also be getting the surgery done and that was the main objective for us—for her to get a permanent hearing implant. Like I said, we spent months going to therapy. They did a lot of exams and tests. Well, on the day that it was her turn to have the surgery, we arrived early in the morning, and they told us that they were not going to be able to do it because Nati had already passed the age limit. Nati was about to turn three years old, and she was not registered at their school—a school that they have where they begin to teach the kids sign language since they are little. We cried so much that day and begged them to do the surgery. For a year we had been working with them, and the expenses we made, all the money we spent with them and with the insurance! It was a lot of money, and it was all for nothing.

"Our family, who really supported us a lot financially, helping us pay for everything, told us to get a lawyer and sue the Center because it wasn't fair. All the trips for the therapy, all for

nothing. I tell you, I had to learn to drive just to take her to those appointments. My husband couldn't miss all of those days of work, so I had to learn to drive. I had no choice. All that time spent driving to therapy. Yes, we cried a lot that day. But, well, what were we going to do? It wasn't possible that day, and that was it. That same day, we canceled the insurance."

The sun had just risen. It was a new day. We were both running late because the traffic at drop-off was out of control. Claudia and I were once again on her couch, ready to go into the next episode of her story. Mostly our meetings had loose topics, but that day we were talking about Nati's health access and her quest to get cochlear implants. This experience was a very vivid memory for Claudia. Within her first year in Houston, she had found a clinic that directed her to a speech center that seemed perfect for Nati's needs. Claudia had survived the border to help her daughter get the services she needed to hear—that was her only mission—and she would do whatever it took to complete it. During our conversations, I noticed that Claudia often said, "What else was I going to do?" At first it sounded like a hopeless question indicating nowhere left to turn, but the more I heard her say it, the more I learned it wasn't that at all. "*¿Qué más podía hacer?*" It wasn't hopelessness; it was, in fact, hope. The last push that Claudia gave to propel herself out of the desert, across the freeway, and into the arms of her daughter was a promise that she would do whatever it took to help her daughter have a better life. There was no other option outside of achieving that. When Claudia said, "What else was I going to do?," she was reminding herself of that promise, setting the course, and stepping out in hope that somehow, no matter how impossible it seemed, she would once again be able to get across that freeway—and every freeway that came after.

"So we went to Memorial Hermann Hospital, where we threw away more money. There the doctor told us she needed one of those tests—you know, the one where they put her in a long tube and she can't move. They put her to sleep with gas so she wouldn't move, and they checked her completely. Pues, ese examen cost us ten thousand dollars, and all of it came from our pocket because we didn't have insurance anymore. They did other tests too. They put little things on her head. We paid for all of it. But we were hopeful because they told us that yes, they could do the surgery. We paid it all because, well, we needed to do the surgery, and the doctor was so positive. He gave us so much hope again. After the exam, they gave us a surgery date and told us to come back. I felt so happy and relieved that my daughter was finally going to get her surgery. But you're not going to believe it. The day we went back for the surgery, the doctor told us it wasn't possible. He said that the hospital didn't have the device they needed, so they couldn't do it. We couldn't believe this was happening to us—again. We begged them not to give up. We even offered . . . well, my husband had found the device online, and we offered to buy it and bring it to the hospital. But the doctor was so cold. He refused and said that he wouldn't risk his license using a device from the 'black market.' Todo cambió así de un día para otro y todo ese dinero nuevamente fue para nada.

"From there, we were paying for everything on our own because the insurance was no longer necessary since she wasn't going to get the surgery. Even after all of that we still spent six months going back to the Speech Center. They told me they were going to help us with therapy, two or three therapies. Anyway, we still had to pay them on our own.

"There was one session during the second therapy where they made loud sounds for her to hear, and the therapist right there told us that as soon as our daughter had the implant, that she would be able to hear. It helped us a lot to know that, so we made an appointment to talk with the audiologist and tell him what the therapist had said. The audiologist wanted the therapist to write a letter saying that our daughter would improve with the surgery. The Speech Center is school, therapist, and clinic. We had to go twice a week, a hundred and fifty dollars per week. So we went back to the therapist, and I asked her for a note. But she told us that she couldn't do that because she didn't want to be held responsible for that.

"I got so angry. There, yes, I did get mad. I told her, 'Why would you tell us that the surgery would help her?' And she told us, 'If they already told you no, then it's no.' Like that! Like if she was scolding a child. I told her, 'Then why are you giving us false hope to keep fighting?' I was so angry I wanted to just cry, but I didn't. I was strong. She said that all we could do was go back to the audiologist and ask her to retest our girl. 'Do all of that again, the same thing, again?' I asked. She was telling us to go through the same process we went through the year before. It was just more of the same.

"I was devastated, but I did it. I went back to the audiologist and asked if we could reapply for the surgery. That time she immediately said no. She said that the doctors all get together and evaluate each kid based on whether they meet the three requirements—they are under three years old, they have an ear-piece on all the time, and they are in the speech therapy school. Well, mine failed two of those requirements, so she said it wasn't possible, but she could give me recommendations for other places we could try.

"So I went to this place on Fannin—I don't even remember anymore what it was called—and they recommended I go back to the Speech Center. I went to two clinics after that, and both clinics sent me back to the Speech Center. Entonces doy vuelta y doy vuelta y caigo donde mismo. And all they say is 'Sorry, but all we can do here is recommend that you go to the Speech Center because that's where they work with kids.' There are other specialists, you know, but that's where they work with kids, so that's where everyone sent me. They even recommended this place all the way out in San Antonio, but it was too complicated for us to go all the way out there. Driving is already dangerous for us. Imagine driving that far. Who knows what might happen? What if we get stopped? What if we get deported on our way there? No. It's just complicated. Allí fue cuando sentimos que nos cortaron las alas y ya no supimos qué hacer."

It was 2015, and Barack Obama was talking about "health care for all." "Hope" was in the air and all over the news. My mom was excited to hear the president talk about making health care more accessible to the uninsured. "Medicaid was good for us," she said. "Can you imagine, with everything we were going through when we got back to the States, if I couldn't take you to the doctor to get your shots for school or to get you checked when you got sick? If it wasn't for Medicaid, I don't know what would have happened to you guys. Thank God, you guys always had good doctors." Both my brother and I were born in public hospitals. Whenever I ask my mom what it was like, she always says it was fine, but that she was so young, she didn't really know what was right or wrong. She doesn't have many things to say about our medical access except that we were always taken care of. She was grateful for Medicaid and other public programs like the Women, Infants, and Children (WIC) program, which also helped our family.

The fact that her children's health access wasn't as memorable for my mom as it was for Claudia speaks to a fundamental difference between them: citizenship. The border had crossed through both of them, and neither had health security, but it wasn't the same. If Claudia had had access to Medicaid for Nati, this episode of her life might have been shorter and less memorable too. According to the Hearing Loss Association of America, Medicaid-eligible children (under age twenty-one) with hearing impairments are entitled to hearing aids and hearing aid services. But undocumented children don't qualify for Medicaid in Texas, so Claudia had to find other ways to help her daughter. She recalled every single dollar amount she paid for Nati's procedures because she and her husband paid them out-of-pocket. Claudia repeatedly emphasized to me how much her insurance cost and when they had it because they paid for it in full—thousands of dollars poured into the health care system by one family for just one child. Claudia's family isn't the only undocumented family that has paid thousands of dollars into the public and private health care systems. Multiply their payments by one million undocumented families: the money speaks for itself.

The idea that immigrants are stealing or wasting public resources is unfounded and, frankly, just cheap xenophobia peddled gratuitously by politicians and the media. Like everyone else at the time, I listened carefully to all of Obama's speeches on health care. I, too, was hopeful for much-needed health care reform and health justice in our country. Hope is a powerful thing like that.

"In another clinic they told us that she could get the surgery, but only when she turns ten," Claudia continued. "So I've just been taking her to checkups, and they do the molds for her ears every four months. It's supposed to be every six months, but her ears grow fast, so she gets them more often. The molds go in her ears so that the sound doesn't leave her ears. They keep the sound in, but when her ear outgrows the mold, that's when the sound escapes, and she hears a zsssiiiiii, and that's when she can't hear anymore. The little bit of sound that reaches her ears . . . well, she can't hear it anymore. That's why the molds are so important.

They've been working with her for years and years, and besides taking her when the devices need maintenance, I also take her to get her ears cleaned. She builds up a lot of wax in her ears, and it's not the yellow wax either. It's this thick, white wax that looks more like Play-Doh that just sticks in there. They've told me I can take her to do a surgery where they place some little tubitos in her ears that helps drain all of that out. Well, yes, it sounds very good, but all of that costs money.

"I still don't understand why she didn't qualify for the surgery. It's been really difficult for us since the Speech Center denied us the surgery because everyone in the city works with them. Everyone sends us to them, and when they don't, they already have Nati's file from the Center. They go based on what the Center tells them, and that's why they don't want to work with us anymore. Everywhere now they have to be ten years old before they can get the surgery.

"We made an appointment at the Children's Hospital to have her tested for the surgery, and it was the first appointment ever that we had to lose. We went on the appointment day, and well, you know, we didn't have insurance, but we had one thousand dollars in cash with us. I said, 'It can't be more than that for the consultation, right?' The receptionist told us that they were going to have her tested that same day, and we said, 'Yes, good,' because, yes, we were going to pay for them, right? But no. That's when se nos doblaron los pies—our feet folded under us. She told us that Nati would need three tests, and that each one of those tests would cost fifteen hundred dollars."

Claudia's gaze fell to the floor; her smile dulled. This particular memory was difficult in a different way. She seemed ashamed. That had been the first time they couldn't make it work financially. Even with all the barriers and disappointments they had endured, through all of it they were proud that no matter how expensive it got, they were able to somehow pool their resources together and pay, in cash, for everything Nati needed. It was a point of pride and a testament to the strength of their family and community. Everyone came together for Nati, no matter what. Claudia and her husband had brought a thousand dollars for Nati's appointment—a lot of money. How could that not be enough? But it wasn't. Not even for one test. But Claudia and her husband shouldn't have felt shame that day or any day. US leaders should be ashamed to continue to uphold a medical system rooted in profit and privilege—a system where medical institutions can charge whatever they want for care and regularly turn people away when they can't pay the outrageous amounts. It wasn't that the family didn't have money. They weren't asking for anything for free. Claudia and her husband had money, money they worked very hard to earn, and that they were ready to give the hospital for their daughter's treatment. The reality is that the hospital didn't want their money; it wanted their dignity and their hope.

"So we canceled, but we tried to reschedule it for another time. The only time they had available was two months away, but we scheduled it. And well, ni modo, we had to come up with the money because she needed the surgery, and we were going to do everything in our power to help our daughter. So she went, and she was tested and seen by specialists. After evaluating her, the specialist there told us that there was a doctor that would do the surgery, but he would have to test Nati again. Y más exámenes. More tests and more tests again, and again, but we told her okay, we will make the sacrifice of paying for these tests all over again if we have to. Because the tests had to be less than six months old, and the ones we had were a year old. And the ones we just did would have worked, but in order to see this other specialist, we would have to wait more than six months because he was on vacation and didn't have any appointments available, entonces no alcanzábamos.

"But like I said, we were going to make the sacrifice even though the doctor told us that she didn't recommend it for Nati. She insisted that Nati was too young at four years old and that we should just leave her this way and wait until she turned ten. She said that they don't like to do the surgery when they are so young because then they don't know how to take care of the device, and they can take it out, and they don't leave it in. I was so tired of hearing this. I got so angry because she didn't know my daughter. I told her that Nati wasn't like everyone else! 'She's not like that,' I said. 'She looks for her devices!' She seeks them out. She seeks out hearing. *¡Busca escuchar! ¡Ella quiere escuchar!*

"There were other reasons too. They didn't want to give her the surgery because they said she had too many languages— English, Spanish, and sign language. They said she had to improve in her sign language because she understood spoken English, but she was still learning signing, the movements, too. I told them that I was taking classes to help her. That I was doing that for her, and she was starting to learn. And you know what they told me? They said, 'Yes, ma'am, but your problem is that you don't speak English.' I felt heartbroken when they said that, and I pleaded with them that I could learn English. 'I know it's not easy, but I can learn!' And they said, 'But while you try to learn, your daughter is falling behind.'"

"Do you believe Nati is falling behind?" I asked.

"No! Not me! She is learning English at school, and I have books that teach sign language in English and Spanish. I can manage! I can pick up the phone and figure it out. My English isn't perfect, but I make the effort. I can translate things quickly, and once I know how it's said, I can teach her. So, no, I don't think she's falling behind because es bien atenta and very smart, and if she doesn't understand me or if I say something wrong, she corrects me! 'Que no se dice así, se dice así,' she tells me.

"So time passed and, well, we didn't take her anymore. We kind of gave up because it was too much money to keep taking her and to keep getting tested and turned down. At one time we even tried to sign up for another insurance, but I think we missed the deadlines to sign up, and it was too late. But then we also thought to keep paying eight hundred dollars a month was too much, and we wanted to at least see if we could find a cheaper policy, but of course for that we had to go back and see the main doctor so that she could give us a referral to the specialist again, and it was just más y más vueltas. So we let it go. We didn't go back. We still take her to the Speech Center, every now and then, to test her to see how she's hearing—if she can hear more or less. I've seen that she's improving. I go into the sound box with her. They make loud sounds, and she has to put a little toy up to her ear. If she hears the sound, she puts the toy on the table, but if she doesn't, she just keeps it on her ear. And me, I cry every time I'm in there with her because I see that she can hear! She says 'Oh!' and puts the toy down. Her face lights up, and she's so happy every time she hears it. How does one not cry?"

In his 2009 health care speech to Congress,[1] President Obama brought people to tears when he described a woman from Texas who "was about to get a double mastectomy when her insurance company cancelled her policy because she forgot to declare a case of acne. By the time she had her insurance reinstated, her breast cancer more than doubled in size. That is heartbreaking, it is wrong," the president emphasized sternly, "and no one should be treated that way in the United States of America." What made this woman's case so heartbreaking was the fact that it was a common story. Across the nation, even people with health insurance did not have health security—a situation that both Claudia and the woman with breast cancer could relate to. In the middle of his speech, however, the president spoke about opponents spreading lies to confuse people and to discredit the Affordable Care Act. One of these lies was that the new reform would include undocumented immigrants. The president looked out at Congress and clearly and succinctly stated: "The reforms that I am proposing will not apply to those that are here illegally." And with that simple phrase, he excluded eleven million people from access to health care. With that simple phrase, the president dragged and wrapped the border around health care once again. With that phrase, he built a wall between Claudia and the Woman From Texas and cut through any possible hope that Claudia's family, or anyone like them, would ever have equal access to quality health care.

The president ended his speech by reading a letter from Ted Kennedy. According to Obama, the letter was meant to remind him that health care "concerns more than material things." "What we face," Kennedy wrote, "is above all a moral issue; at stake are not just the details of policy, but fundamental principles of social justice and the character of our country." Well, the character of our country had spoken. Universal health care didn't come. "Esperanzas falsas," as Claudia said, was all we were left holding. Just false hope.

Claudia told me that they had spent more than $30,000 trying to get Nati cochlear implants. Several doctors saw Nati and gave them false hope, convinced them to pay for redundant tests and happily took their money, only to turn them away at the very end. When telling this part of her story, Claudia would often pause to cry remembering the utter despair and anger she felt every time they were turned away. I couldn't help thinking that if Nati were a US citizen—maybe if Nati weren't Mexican—maybe she would not have had to go through any of that. She would have had her surgery, and it wouldn't have caused her family so much emotional and financial hardship. Claudia had walked across the border and into an unjust medical system that preyed on her hopes and aspirations as an immigrant, as a mother, as a person determined to do anything to help her daughter.

I also couldn't help but think of the history of medical experimentation on Mexican and immigrant women and girls conducted by racist scientists during the time of eugenics in the United States—experiments used only to tag and label them as pathological, incompetent, unworthy, not enough, or too much. Medical practices that traumatized an entire population for generations. Nati was somehow always "perfect" for endless medical exams, but then simultaneously "too young" and "too old" for the treatment that she actually needed. Nati had too many languages. Nati didn't have enough language. Nati was too much of this, not enough of that. It's tragic how these specialists had no problem doing tests and charging Nati's family thousands of dollars, but found all the "problems" when it came to actually treating her.

How does a hospital not have a necessary device at the last minute? Why would a hospital charge a family thousands of dollars for tests and consultations to prepare for a specific surgery without knowing if they could actually do the surgery? This is the kind of exploitation that is facilitated by medical marginalization and exclusion. This is the kind of legalized theft that happens when health care is ruled by profit. These are the kinds of inhumane, immoral, and predatory practices that undocumented immigrants, and other (im)migrants, are exposed to simply because they don't have a Social Security number. And how is it possible to have "too many languages" anyway? Maybe if Claudia wasn't so Mexican, if her Spanish wasn't so perfect, maybe then Nati would have cochlear implants—too Mexican, too uninsured, too undocumented, too other.

"She can hear better from her right ear," Claudia continued. "From the left ear she can't really hear anything. I can tell the difference when they do the tests. They do them with the machine and without, and I can always tell the difference. Therapy is to learn how to listen and speak. They also take her out of class for half an hour one day and then again another, so she goes twice a week. Twice a week one teacher takes her to work on speaking, and another teacher takes her to work on listening and making sentences. I want her to be independent because she's always been so independent, ever since she was a baby. But in the regular class the teacher can't give her special attention, and that's what the other teachers do. They give her special attention. They go over the most commonly used words. They make sure she knows when the teacher gives her commands like 'Leave your backpack,' 'Take out your book,' 'Sit down,' 'Read your book,' 'Read this to me and then go sit down,' or anything like that where she has to follow directions. In that aspect the teachers have helped me so much. The speech teacher helps her a lot too. She teaches her to make sounds like 'ahhh,' but in English, right? But she learns it with her vocal cords and her hands—'ahhh, mmm'—and she has to make the sounds because all she says is 'ahhh,' and that's all, but she has advanced a lot. She says 'Mamá,' 'Papá,' 'agua,' 'luna,' 'Juan.' Esas palabritas ya me las dice. She can already say those little words. She struggles a little, right? But she always gets it. I am grateful to the school for this because they have helped her a lot.

"But I need to go to the school to talk with someone because the teacher we have now is not good at communicating with me. I have to go ask for a meeting with the main teacher and with her sign language teacher. Because I go in to talk to them, and they tell me that I have to show her pictures and have her give me a sentence, but I don't like that. I feel like that is making her fall behind. I don't want her to learn to look at pictures because she's not always going to have a picture, but then she's going to want a picture all the time, and that's not right. She is capable of reading the letters and identifying them. She can do it. But if she's always waiting for the picture, she's not going to know what's going on, and that's what I don't want.

"I had this whole wall, on this side, covered in papers all over the place." Claudia points to the wall next to her, beside the dinner table. The dining room opens to the living room, so I can see the wall from the couch. It's blank but there are school papers on the table. "I had the letters of the alphabet in capital and lowercase, the numbers, the numbers in written form, and this is where we put them up. It's where we still put them up. Actually, I just took them all down because I thought, It looks very messy, and . . . well, she's not a baby anymore, but I always take the papers out, and we still practice every day. I tell her, 'Come on, tell me.' I put up letters and she has to form the words for me. No sabe ni que—she doesn't know what's going on—but when she tells me a sentence, then she can remember the words. She doesn't say anything, but she tries—she tries to form the sentences and tries to remember the words. I can see she remembers.

"I'm going to go back in time a little. When she was only two, she couldn't walk. It was for the same reason that she couldn't hear. When you can't hear, your balance is off, because that's where your body's balance is, in your ears. So she couldn't walk, and at school they taught her how to walk, to climb stairs, because she couldn't do any of that. This was in preschool, right? That school helped us a lot too, but Nati also fell behind at that school. I think it's because all they did there was play, just play and draw and sing songs and move their hands and move their feet. She didn't learn anything useful there, not like what she is learning in her school now. Here she's learning to write more and know more things y pos si, así es mejor."

I couldn't help but smile a little. In addition to the clear concerns for Nati's hearing impairment, I could also hear the underlying Mexican, immigrant mother realness in this part of Claudia's story. Nati was in preschool and just a baby, but Claudia was not happy about her wasting time playing and singing songs; she wanted to see her working hard. I could hear and see my grandmother, my mother, and myself in these words—the urge to see our children do well, be accepted, succeed, to make sure they wouldn't suffer "like we did," my grandmother says. It's a full commitment to the whole child. It's culture; it's habitus; it's habit.

How do we transfer the sacrifices we have made and the suffering we have endured to our children? We push them to be better, "so that you never have to work as hard as I did," my mother says. I understood the aspiration, the stakes, in Claudia's effort to make sure Nati stays as "independent" as she's always been. Her frustration with the school making things "too easy" for Nati by giving her visual aids made sense. Claudia knew that Nati would always be held to higher standards, that she would always have to work harder and be better and stronger than her peers if she was going to make it in the world—not just because of her hearing, but also because of her political status, her race, her gender, all of it. Given all the medical struggles Nati encountered, it was very clear to Claudia what her daughter needed.

"¡Ay, Dios! . . . Es muy difícil. Si se enferma, allí voy. Si se enferma la otra, allí voy también. If she gets sick, there I go. If the other one gets sick, there I go again. I used to take English classes. Well, right now the semester has ended, but I took computer classes at ten o'clock at night. I would take them through video chat. I did it so that I could get better and help her more, right? So I could teach her the words and the signs. I teach her signs, and she teaches me signs. But for everything she needs, it's me. Everything . . . it's just me. I'm her interpreter. I'm even the interpreter for my husband."

Claudia's voice began to break. She paused for a few seconds, quietly wiping away tears. "Es muy difícil ser la única. My husband works all day. He leaves at 6:30 a.m. and gets home at 7:30 p.m., sometimes later. Él ayuda, aportando dinero, ¿verdad? No digo que no, pero no más. I have to be her everything. Pero es mi niña, es de mi y yo de ella. She is my girl. She is of me and I of her, and I've learned so much from her. Everything that I've learned, I've learned from her." Claudia paused.

"I knew when I was over there that I couldn't do it." Her voice kept breaking as she continued, sometimes sobbing, and there were long pauses, but Claudia tried to talk through her tears. "Before, when she was a baby, and it felt really difficult, I used to say . . . um . . . I would say . . . um . . . I'm really crazy, right? . . . But I would say, 'Diosito, why did you send me a child like this? I didn't do anything wrong.' I don't want you to think bad of me. Es que . . . sometimes I thought I couldn't do it anymore. Me desesperaba mucho, mucho. I would get frustrated, desperate, and I would scold her y la regañaba, '¡Es que porque tú!' And, of course, she would just stare at me. She didn't understand anything. In time, I learned not to yell at her. Yes, sometimes I still speak to her fuerte, sternly, but I speak to her like a normal child. I want you to know that today I don't feel the same as I used to before. Today I say, 'Thank you, God, for sending me this child.' And, no, it's not a punishment. Um . . . I know that with her I was a bit descarriada, wayward, but with her I have learned so much."

I gave Claudia space to cry—to feel what she needed to feel without asking anything or interrupting her story. Was it guilt, shame, sadness, regret, exhaustion, depression? Maybe it was some combination, or all of them, or something else. Claudia could barely speak through the tears. As I listened to her, I thought about all the times I had lost patience with my children, the times I also scolded and demanded more than they could give or even comprehend, the times I felt despair and unworthiness as a mother.

"I'm really crazy, right?" Claudia said. I, too, have felt crazy, especially when I was struggling with postpartum depression. Claudia had not been to therapy but used prayer as one way to find solace and as a place to relieve her grief. Children's needs are always immediate, and that can be overwhelming sometimes. I think most mothers can relate. A lot of factors were compounded for Claudia though. Raising a child is a lot of work, but added to that was the stress of dealing with doctors, language specialists, and various school demands as a recent immigrant just starting to learn the language and politically excluded from many resources.

Claudia's suffering was rooted in the very real and difficult situations she was living, and yet, the weight of maternal guilt and grief she carried was also real. It was clear from the outpouring of tears and long pauses that sharing her story wasn't easy. "I don't want you to think bad of me," Claudia stressed. Most mothers are afraid of being judged and socially condemned for having any feelings other than absolute joy and gratitude for their children. But mothers can love and be grateful for their children and still feel tired, even overwhelmed and ready to give up sometimes. Mothering isn't always joyful. All mothers, including undocumented immigrants, are human and, as such, are allowed to feel the entire spectrum of emotions about motherhood.

I don't have a child with a disability, and I recognize that I don't know what it's like to raise a child with a disability. But I do know what maternal guilt feels like; I know what it sounds like. I know how profoundly painful and all-consuming it can be. I hated seeing Claudia feel that. I wanted to tell her that it was okay. I wanted to tell her not to cry, but I wanted her to cry if she needed to. I got up and sat next to her. I gave her a hug and just tried to hold space. I was honored that she would be so vulnerable with me and share something so intimate with all of us. In sharing parts of my story, I try to share the burden of that vulnerability. All I can do is hope that the reader will do the same. After a long embrace, Claudia continued her story.

"I'm not going to tell you I've been an exemplary mother, right? But, um . . . I've gotten better. She's made me better. Es una experiencia bonita, a la vez bonita y a la vez difícil. Not sad, difficult, because there are so many obstacles. There are obstacles where you say to yourself, 'How am I going to do that?' For example, a mi se me complica mucho ir a la escuela. It's complicated for me to go to a meeting, to ask the teachers a question. 'Maestra, ¿qué van a traer mañana?' 'Maestra, ah, ¿qué trabajos le dejo?' '¿Como se portó la niña?' Hablan puro inglés, y es cuando se me dificulta. Sometimes I just want to say, 'Teacher, my daughter forgot her notebook,' something quick, you know?

But I have to stop and think, How do I say that? So I look for Beatriz. Beatriz is my translator. Beatriz will grab me and say, 'Come on, hurry up, let's go ask!' But, well, I can't always be with her, right? So sometimes I try to find a teacher that speaks Spanish or someone that could translate for me right then, but when there's no one, ¿pues quién, verdad? So a lot of times I would just say, 'Okay, ya así está bien. Never mind.' Y mejor me quedaba con la duda. And I would just stay with the doubt. Oh, but when the teacher has a complaint about my daughter, two times they will call me with a complaint, and there they sure do find a translator for that, de bolada.

"Por eso te digo que para todo, soy yo, sola. I have to deal with everything by myself. I have learned a lot, but it's still hard, and when I think I can't do it, I have to be my own emotional support, yo misma me enojo, lloro y me encontento. Porque, sí, a veces me da mucho coraje. Sometimes I do get really angry, because [my husband] . . . well, there are all the doctors, and this and that. And when does this need to be done? And how much do they charge? And is there something cheaper? Porque yo le busco—I search around—so that I know that I can pay. Or I have to make sure that they're good, and I have to ask, 'What are the risks? How many? What else?' And for everything, it's me! I'm the one that's calling everyone.

"So yes, sometimes I get mad. I want him to be there with me, to feel that he's supporting me. Pero he doesn't support me. He just stays silent. It's not that he doesn't want to help. I don't think it's that. Well, yes and no. He is more sensitive than me. If the doctor tells him . . . if the doctor gives him one no, he starts to cry. If I'm sensitive, he's worse. He doesn't say a lot—for anything, right? But just lagrimotas."

"And you're not like that?" I asked.

"Well, yes, I am like that too. ¡Yo también quiero llorar, pero me lo trago como dicen por allí! I want to cry too, but I eat it, and I keep asking the doctors questions. I don't just accept the first no. Yes, it is sad. It's sad and painful, but I have to keep fighting for my daughter. I can feel that it's difficult for her, but I'm still proud of her. I feel very proud of my daughter. If a mother is proud of her daughter, I feel even prouder of mine!"

3 | WHAT SICKNESS?

"RIGHT NOW, I AM SICK. I HAVE A SICKNESS QUE YA NO se quita. It's a sickness in my bones. I get sudden pains in my joints. Some days it's worse than others, but the pain is always there. Despite that, I still get up at five in the morning and make lunch for my daughters, bathe them, and take them to school. Everything. A lot of times I just have to do it all like that, with pain and everything. And my mind, for example, has to say, '¿Cuál enfermedad? What sickness?' because I have obligations."

I had to push Claudia to talk about her own health. I had to keep prepping her, reminding her I was going to ask about it. It wasn't the first question I asked because it couldn't be. I learned this in conversations with other mothers. First I had to give Claudia the time and space to tell me everything that was most important to her, and that was her children. Only after she had the chance to talk about her struggles to find care for Nati was Claudia ready to even approach the subject of her own health, and even then, the story was much shorter, truncated, and interrupted by what Claudia said was "forgetfulness."

It was a new day. Claudia and I were on a different couch. In the little time that had passed since our last conversation, her family had moved. The new house wasn't far from their previous home. Nati was still at the same school, but Claudia was excited about the significant differences in her new space. Her previous home was a two-bedroom apartment in a small complex with maybe only five other units. There was a shared outdoor space that Claudia utilized well, despite the size. I remember it being carefully set up with four long tables decorated with colorful centerpieces from the *Trolls* movie. There was a bouncy house on one end of the yard and a taco station on the other. It was Nati's birthday, and I remember being excited that Claudia was as passionate about birthday parties as I am. Going all out for a birthday party felt very Mexican to me because that's how I grew up. I felt a connection.

Claudia's new home was much bigger. It was a house with a lot more land. They had large front and back yards where Claudia had already set up hammocks and toys for her girls to play and enjoy the space. She was excited to show me all of the details of her new home. Claudia boasted about how spacious and bright the inside of her house was. Natural light in a home is very important to me too, so I understood her excitement. We talked a while about the move and how things still weren't completely in their place, but everything was new and exciting. Normal new house, moving stuff. I was happy for Claudia. Even though she emphasized the joy the space would bring to her girls, I could tell it was also a ray of hope for her. We settled onto the new couch in the large, bright living room, the baby quietly watching cartoons in the other room.

"One day the pain was so strong," Claudia went on. "It was so bad, I had to make my husband take a day off work to take care of the girls so that I could go cure myself. It wasn't too long ago, maybe a few months ago. I was making tortillas, and the pain hit me hard in the lower part of my body. So then, well, he didn't go to work because I couldn't even stand up! I couldn't stand. My stomach was swollen, and my whole lower part got really bad. So, yes, I'm a little sick, but . . . I stay silent because I don't have anyone to take care of my daughters, especially the little one, or because we don't have money. I have obligations, y no puedo ir, I can't go, y así verdad.

"The sickness in my bones is, um . . . it's called fibro . . . fibro . . . um . . ."

"Fibromyalgia?" I asked.

"Yes, something like that. They just discovered I had it like five months ago. I went to the doctor because I didn't feel well. I felt really bad. I would get a lot of fevers, and I had so much pain in my bones. I would get chills, and I just couldn't stand it. My head would hurt so bad, I would get hit with a pain here, and then this whole side of my body would hurt. Pues, sí, me sentía muy mal. I had been feeling that way for a long time, so one day I just said, 'No! No more!' I was driving and the headache hit me, and I felt dizzy like I wanted to vomit and pass out. So that was when I went to the doctor and told him everything I was feeling. The doctor gave me some medicine, and at first it helped control the pain, and I thought, Okay, now I will feel better. But with my body . . . my body just wouldn't receive the treatment. The medicine makes me shake a lot, and it makes me nauseous and gives me headaches. I didn't like taking it because it would make me speak incoherently. It's like it drugs me up too much, muy feo, because of the pain, it drugs me up really bad. So I stopped taking it for a couple of weeks, but then the pain came back again, so I had to go back to it. I started taking it at night, just one time, and that helped for a little while. But now I've noticed that it stopped working."

According to the Centers for Disease Control and Prevention, common symptoms of fibromyalgia are pain and stiffness all over the body, headaches and migraines, fatigue, tingling or numbness, digestive issues, depression, and anxiety. Claudia recalled that she had been diagnosed with fibromyalgia only a few months before our conversation. It made me wonder how long she may have been dealing with the symptoms, how long she'd gone undiagnosed, and how fibromyalgia may have affected her mothering in the months after she first arrived in the United States. As I did more research on the illness, I read that there weren't really any definitive answers as to what might cause fibromyalgia, but there are some theories and associations. Most of the publications I read concluded that symptoms of fibromyalgia often begin after a traumatic physical or psychological experience, and women are more likely to develop it.

I thought back to Claudia's migration story: the desperation she felt to leave, fleeing everything and everyone she knew, the multiple failed attempts to cross the river, the fear of drowning, all the times she had to say goodbye to Nati and leave her with coyotes, the fear of what might happen and of possibly never seeing her daughter again, the guilt of putting her in the care of strangers. I thought about how Claudia's body was shoved into the roof fairing of an eighteen-wheeler truck, the terror she felt when she was caught and left in the desert with a strange man, and then threatened with death and rape by the people who were supposed to get her safely across the border. I thought about her being caught by Immigration and thrown in a detention center—the fear of being erased, of having no way to contact her family and call for help, the extreme cold, and the humiliation of not having the privacy to fulfill basic human needs such as using the bathroom.

Even after all of that, she kept trying to cross. She had to for Nati. I thought about how Claudia was stuffed inside of another truck with dozens of other people she didn't know, mostly men, crammed in like sardines. How she had to listen to a woman being raped and wait in horror to see if she would be next. How she had to try as hard as she could to be quiet and invisible so she wouldn't be caught by Immigration, and so she wouldn't stand out to the men. I thought about her walking across the desert in the middle of the night, stepping over cadavers and snakes, terrified of lagging and getting separated from the group, her feet destroyed, bleeding and blistered, exhausted and barely able to walk. Yes, I thought to myself, that sounds like a pretty traumatic physical and psychological experience or, rather, experiences—multiple, repeated, concentrated.

The body records trauma. The collateral damage of migration, the shock, was forever carved into Claudia's body. I think about how it would feel to have anything carved into my body. Of course it would hurt, but would the pain linger and vibrate for days? Years? Would I feel the pain deep in my bones, in my joints—the parts of my body that stitch me together and make me whole? Would I get migraines and get so overwhelmed by the pain that I would fall into deep despair, into depression? I don't think Claudia made the connection between her fibromyalgia symptoms and her migration. When I asked her if she ever thought about it, she seemed surprised at first, then pensive, like maybe it made sense. "Pero, ¿quién sabe, verdad?" she asked, as though a connection had been made, but it was all too much to think about.

Another word for trauma can be *susto*. My grandmother took susto very seriously. She taught me that when you experience a traumatic event, your spirit is jolted out of your body, frightened away, leaving you disoriented and vulnerable. If you don't take care to recover your frightened spirit, your body remains defenseless, open, and more susceptible to additional harm—including illness. Over and over, Claudia referred to her migration story as horrible, "muy feo." I think she understood that it was a traumatizing experience, but from what she shared with me, she hadn't named the trauma, the susto, or taken the time to begin healing her spirit, to call it back to her body.

Claudia couldn't really say how long she'd experienced the symptoms of fibromyalgia, but she was sure it started after she migrated to the United States. I thought about her revelation of feeling overwhelmed and hopeless as Nati's mother and sole caregiver. Seemingly disparate parts of her story were beginning to connect; the physical body of trauma was forming like a puzzle, coming into view with each intangible piece. For years Claudia had been suffering from the symptoms of fibromyalgia, feeling chronic and invasive pain all over her body while also fighting with doctors to obtain care for her daughter, worrying about how she would pay for everything, and being tortured by migraines, nausea, and dizziness. But despite everything, she was also learning how to mother a strong and independent daughter with a hearing disability, and learning how to adapt to and align with all of the demands of a North American life, including learning English and American Sign Language, teaching her daughter both of those as well as Spanish, dealing with teachers and physicians who questioned her motherhood because of the language she spoke (or didn't speak), while also being undocumented and feeling burdened by the numerous barriers and threats she faced just driving her children to the doctor.

To say that she was dealing with a lot is an understatement. It's more than most of us could handle. It's enough to make the physical body crash and scream for help. Fibromyalgia was Claudia's body screaming for help, begging her to stop and heal, begging someone to help her stop and heal. Fibromyalgia literally knocked Claudia off her feet. It made it impossible for her to do anything, even walk. It made her, for the first time, demand that her husband help her.

Illness is the body communicating to us, and everyone around us, that something is wrong, and we need to listen. Sometimes the body whispers, but other times it shouts. Because everything else is noisy and demanding, the body must be louder, especially for women. It makes sense to me, given all the demands and pressures on women and mothers, that women are more likely to get an illness characterized by chronic, generalized pain all over the body. It makes sense, given how uncompromising the demands on women are, that women would be more likely to get an illness that makes their bodies cry in pain and shut down in protest. I wonder how many undocumented immigrant women might be suffering from undiagnosed fibromyalgia. How many might suffer from depression and anxiety caused by fibromyalgia? Biomedicine doesn't know the exact cause of the disease because there isn't just one cause located in the material body. It can't be dissected out of a person and biopsied. It doesn't fit under a microscope or in a test tube. We may never know how many undocumented Latinas suffer from fibromyalgia or other stress-induced illnesses—from the strain and complexity of an undocumented life compounded by gendered demands, chronic pain, and the stigma of an invisible illness, screaming but unheard.

"My whole body hurts. Todo," Claudia went on. "But I don't think the doctor is helping. Sometimes I don't think they believe me, or they think it's just in my head. He hasn't told me to stop eating anything or given me any other solutions. He just tells me to exercise a lot. So I go and exercise every day, but I have to wear knee braces because my knees hurt so much. I mostly just go to Zumba, but here at the house, when I'm home with my girls, I do some things too. My husband bought me some cositas so that . . . so that I could also do some exercises here in the house whenever I could. ¿Se siente feo, sabes? The pain is the worst. The pain in my hips and in my knees. That's what I feel most often, the pain in those parts of my body. Sometimes in, all over, I can't even say where, in my shoulders, here and there, in the fingers of my hand, here, all over. It feels awful. It's awful because you're just standing, you know, just standing there and fúm, all of a sudden, se te afloja el pie, your foot gives out, and it hurts you. It hurts you. Or you want to walk. . . . There are times that I kneel, and I don't get up anymore because I can't. And I'm not good at kneeling because then I have to crawl over to something I can grab on to in order to bring myself back up. Because my knees and hips hurt so much. Entonces se siente feo estar así.

"The medicines the doctor gives me are for the pains. I take them every day. All of this is for life now, por vida. Two weeks ago, I went back to the doctor, right? Because the pills weren't working anymore. So he had to prescribe me a much, much stronger medication. I have to take them, but I don't like to take them because they are so strong that they are hitting me hard. And I know that I will get used to them, and then one day they will stop working, and then there won't be any other pills that will help because that was the limit. None. So I really didn't want a stronger dose, but they had to increase it because I felt the same. Pain, dizziness, y pa'allá y pa'acá y me la tuvieron que subir. I have no choice but to take them because if I don't take them, for sure I will be in constant pain. Everything. Everything. And if I stop taking it one or two days, I'll start back again with the shaking, fever, pain, y pa'allá y pa'acá, that is why I have to take them every day. Every day. Every night because in the morning I forget everything, but at night for sure I remember to take them. If not, I carry them in my purse, and I also carry Tylenol just in case I can't stand the pain, or if I get hit with sudden pains, then I take a Tylenol."

As I was listening to Claudia, I was thinking about how hard she was trying to feel better. There wasn't any room in her day for chronic pain. She had too much to do. I felt a pull in my gut imagining Claudia crawling around a room, alone, in pain, trying to pull herself up. Her concern that the doctors didn't believe her pain, that they might think "it's all in her head," wasn't at all far-fetched. There is a long history of women's pain being dismissed or ignored by doctors—and of doctors rejecting women's complaints of physical pain and attributing their symptoms to psychosis/hysteria instead. Gender bias in medicine, like racial bias, doesn't look like a doctor calling a woman hysterical and sending her home. It can look like a woman pleading that she's in unbearable physical pain, that her knees ache, and the doctor telling her to exercise more.

There are other factors that would also render Claudia's pain invisible to US doctors. Her comment that the doctor just insisted that she needed to "exercise more" kept replaying in my mind. I couldn't shake the connections. In my research I had found more than a few instances of doctors pushing uninsured Latina patients to "be more responsible" for their own health. Feeding them a particularly paternalistic formula of "Do better" individualism and acute personal responsibility that had become common in health care, but that always seemed to be especially cocked, loaded, and ready to shoot at the working poor and uninsured patients of color.

Besides the multiple biases in her medical encounters, Claudia was also experiencing the stigma of having a chronic illness that wasn't physically evident—of feeling pain that altered her state of being and limited her functioning, but that nobody could see or understand. "Se siente feo," Claudia said over and over, lacking the words to describe the depth of her suffering. I also lack the words, and society lacks words, and sympathy, for these kinds of experiences. People like Claudia might get an initial recognition of their suffering, but after a while, with no proof of disability, that sympathy withers away in the face of the demands of the day, the demands of "normalcy." The children have to be cared for, the food has to be made, the house has to be cleaned—and Claudia has to do it. Period. "Es por vida," Claudia lamented. She would have to struggle with the debilitating symptoms of fibromyalgia every day for the rest of her life, performing nor-malcy, to get through the day, and all she had were painkillers and Zumba.

"I don't have financial assistance," Claudia emphasized again, as though reading my thoughts. "I have to pay for everything myself. Every doctor visit costs me sixty-five dollars, just to see the doctor, but then if they send you to do a special test or to the laboratory, well then . . . almost every time I go, I spend at least three hundred dollars, and that doesn't include the medicine.

There's no financial assistance there. It's not a community clinic. I don't go there anymore because I never qualify. I used to go to a community clinic. In this one, I was being treated. That's where they discovered I had cancer cells en el cuello uterino. I had to have part of my ... part of my cervix removed. That happened about two years ago. Then another cyst returned but not the cancer cells, so now I just have cysts, quistes, en la matriz. I have eight. Four here and four there. Now I'm taking medicine para que se me desbaraten solos, so that they will fall apart on their own. There at that clinic, at first, I did qualify for financial assistance because my husband had lost hours at work and, um, he was making very little. But now he's making a little more, thank God, but in order to qualify he has to make less than two thousand dollars a month, and well, now he makes a little more than that. And that's why we say that one has to be dying in order to qualify for anything. So I stop my treatment because we just don't have money sometimes. My husband's salary changes all the time. Sometimes we are okay, and sometimes we're not. Right? So sometimes I will go without treatment, and then when I can, I will go back. I was just able to start again two weeks ago, so I'm being treated now."

Claudia had just revealed that in addition to fibromyalgia, she had part of her cervix surgically removed due to cancer, but she was still having symptoms of recurring cysts. Listening to her calmly move into her history of cervical cancer and her partial hysterectomy, while I was still trying to wrap my mind around the compounding symptoms of fibromyalgia she was experiencing, forced me to pause.

It wasn't just the fibromyalgia but the combination of illnesses and Claudia's matter-of-fact demeanor that jolted me back to memories of my mom, and how Mexican women resist talking about illness and pain and the things that almost kill them.

When I was around fifteen years old, my mom had a hysterectomy. I vaguely remember her talking about it afterwards with my aunt, who also had one several years later. At the time, I never asked my mom about it—how she felt or what it was like. Another difficult conversation I had waited too long to have.

"When the doctor told me I had to have my uterus removed, I immediately said, 'No way,'" my mom recalled. "I had gone to the doctor because I was having really heavy periods, and I found out I was anemic from how much I was bleeding. I remember one time I was at the taqueria working and I sat down, and when I got up, ¡habia manchado todo de sangre! I thought maybe my period had just started, but it was scary. I had stained the whole chair with blood. I had not been going to the doctor because I didn't have insurance. So it wasn't so easy to just go all the time. Pero un día, I just decided to go to one of those free clinics. It was so long ago, I don't remember what it was called, but they checked me and told me I had a swollen uterus, que la matriz estaba inflamada, inflamed, and that it needed to come out. I said, 'No. No way.' I don't even know why I reacted like that. I didn't know anything about what could happen if you had your uterus removed. I just knew . . . I just felt it in my gut that I did not want to do that. So I left.

"I kept having heavy periods. Yes, now that I think about it, I remember I was always so tired back then, but I never thought anything of it because we had the two taquerias, and I was working all the time. I just thought it was stress from all the work. But one time we were in Mexico with your padrinos, and we went to these caves in San Luis, and we swam all the way to the bottom, and I remember that when I was coming back up, I got very, very dizzy and almost passed out. I have never experienced that thing where you feel like you are going to faint, but this time I did. I felt that I was going to faint. Nomás, that your dad grabbed me and helped me. They gave me some water and I felt better. But that's when your dad said, 'Let's go see a doctor here in Mexico.' I already knew I was bleeding too much, and I wanted a second opinion anyway, so we went.

"The doctor in Mexico said that he couldn't believe I was still alive! 'I don't know how you haven't had a heart attack yet,' he said. ¡Y me regañó! Because my anemia was so high. He told me the same thing as the American doctor—that my uterus was swollen and that's why I was bleeding so much, and that I would have to take it out. He said he could give me medicine for the anemia but that after a while it wouldn't do anything because it was just going to get worse. I would keep having the hemorrhages. But I told him the same thing. I said no. I was so scared to have that done. I didn't know why, but I just thought, They're taking out an entire part of me, and that can't be good. That has to do something to you. I just had this sense that it was dangerous, you know, and I didn't want to do it. The doctor kept telling me that I didn't have anything to worry about, that I would be the same because they weren't going to remove my ovaries. Fíjate, I didn't even know it was about the ovaries. That the ovaries were the most important part. Because I had heard that if they take your uterus out that you change. You get old and wrinkle faster, like you stop being a woman or something. But the doctor said that I didn't need my uterus anymore if I wasn't going to have babies. I was only what? Thirty-five, thirty-six. I didn't want to have any more babies, but I didn't know anything else either. I didn't know what it would do to me. And having my uterus removed, yo sentía que iba estar hueca. I thought I would be hollow. The doctor told me that in the future, la matriz inflamada could cause more fibroids, because they had also found a small fibroid, and that it could even cause cancer. So we went back home, and I was thinking about it and talking with other women. I talked with Jane, and you know how she is."

Jane is an older white woman whose home my mother cleaned for years. She called herself my mom's "Jewish mother." Because my mom was very young when she started working for her, Jane had become a kind of maternal figure. "Jane was just like, 'Get over it!'" my mom recalled. "'You don't need it anymore! What do you want it for? Let it go.' Pero las gringas son diferentes. Ya sabes como son. They see it different. La matriz para nosotras es. . . . No sé. No sé. . . . Es importante. It's not like your appendix or something like that. It's different. Our uterus is important to us.

"I went back to that clinic I had gone to the first time, and they sent me to St. Mary's Hospital, I think. I was lucky because at that time they had a program to help women like me that didn't have insurance and couldn't pay. So I did the surgery there in that hospital. I ended up doing it because I was worried about how much I was bleeding, and I didn't want to keep feeling sick.

I remember after I came out, I was in a room with other women because it was a charity hospital, so they had a lot of women in one room. There was a Black woman in a bed next to me, and she goes, 'Yeah, I had the whole damn thing taken out. I said, "Get it all out. I don't want to have any issues with this thing!"' There was another woman in there too, and I remember she kept clicking that pain medicine they give you after surgeries. What is it called? I don't remember, but I never clicked that thing, not once! Ni una vez me puse esa medicina. ¡Me hice macha! I don't know, I had heard that people get addicted to that stuff and I thought, Pobre y luego queriendo drogas, ¡pos, no!

"But I wish I had known more back then. I didn't know anything, so I didn't ask. I heard now, I heard on the radio, that you don't need to have your uterus removed anymore. ¡Fíjate! Why do they just now discover that? I wish I had the option back then because I still regret it. I would not have done it if I thought I had another option. It was hard for me at the time. I felt sad because I had to take care of myself those days after the surgery. Your dad was working all day at the taqueria, and your grandma was working too. I was at home by myself."

I hadn't thought to ask my mom how she felt about having a hysterectomy because it didn't feel like a big deal at the time. I was maybe fifteen. She seemed the same to me, still working and taking care of everything. At the time, my mom and dad owned a taco truck and a small taqueria. The businesses weren't doing well. In fact, the taquerias went under right around the time I turned seventeen. So when my mom says she was stressed at the time she found out she had a swollen uterus and deadly anemia, she was putting it lightly. When I sat down to ask her about the hysterectomy, I found out how deeply it had affected her sense of self, and how worried she'd been throughout the whole ordeal. My mom always seemed to take life as it came and rarely complained about anything she was feeling. She some-times got stressed about everyday things, like anyone else, but she always gave off this feeling of "things are as they should be." So I often believed her. I feel bad for not knowing, and for being too lost in my own annoyed teenage world, mad about having to spend my weekends bussing tables at the taqueria, to see that she was dealing with so much. I think now about how many hours she worked on her feet making tacos, serving tables, scrubbing showers and vacuuming floors, raising three kids— all while hemorrhaging. I think about how the doctor said she could've had a heart attack at any moment. How she could've just passed out one day and never gotten up again. I think about how she didn't know she was in danger because she was so used to working so hard that feeling exhausted and weak was normal for her.

Why would Claudia just have a partial hysterectomy and risk the possibility of the cancer returning, or risk dealing with cysts her whole life? On the one hand, she still wanted to have more children. On the other, for Claudia, as for my mother, the womb is sacred; the power to create life is what gave them their place and purpose, what made them feel whole, not "hollow," as my mom put it. Claudia, like my mom, would risk lifetime pain, bleeding, and abnormal growths rather than lose her life source. It doesn't have to make sense to anyone else: it's embodied life, an intimate relationship to one's own body and life purpose. Even my mom couldn't really explain it to me. It was just a gut feeling for her. My mom is not a very religious person, and as a Chicana she had her own sense of mexicanidad. If you asked her, she would never call herself a marianista, or any of the other words that have been used to label "Latina reproductive behavior" as exotic and pathological. I know that's what you're thinking, reader, but you need to pause and allow space for alternative possibilities—allow space for all the complex and complicated relationships women have to their bodies and their wombs.

As I was listening to Claudia and reflecting on my mom, and listening to my mom and reflecting on Claudia, I was brought back to myself. What did this all mean for me? I asked my mom if she thought a swollen uterus, fibroids, hemorrhages, and hysterectomies were genetic in our family. Had any of the doctors suggested it? Did I have to worry about this? Of course I did. I flashed back to both of my labors. I hemorrhaged after both, and each time medical staff had to scramble to help me because none of us knew this about my medical history. During my daughter's birth, I bled so much, I passed out and woke up to my midwife yelling, "Do not die on me!" I thought about how it took me three years to conceive my second child because my uterus was so full of polyps. I thought about my long history of heavy periods, and how the ayurvedic doctor I visited a couple of times called me a "bleeder." She said that blood was an important part of my medical and spiritual past and that I had to honor and accept that if I really wanted to heal. *Uterus* in Spanish is *matriz*; it means center point, headquarters, where it all begins and ends, place of knowledge and safety, womb, matrix, connection, flow, source. The ayurvedic doctor suggested that I donate blood every now and then to release some of the blood, and thus tension, in my body. Blood donation was one modern and legal form of bloodletting, she explained. There was an entire medical history, undocumented and yet pointedly marked, in the deeply personal memories of my mother's past, stowed away in stories about things that seemed so unrelated and disconnected. I had to go through her migration, cross the border again with her, to get to her reproductive health, to get back to her womb and then mine.

In many ways the truncated nature of Claudia's illness narrative reflects the unpredictable nature of her health access or lack of access. It was the same for my mom, who prefaced her narrative with "It was so long ago, I don't even remember most of it." So I find myself filling in the gaps a bit more on this one, taking the liberty to emphasize, accentuate, and highlight that Claudia, like my mother, was carrying a lot, and that this heavy load is something that most mothers carry. Claudia didn't know that Latinas have the highest rate of cervical cancer in the country. Neither did my mom. In many ways Claudia was lucky she caught the cancer in time and had it removed; a lot of women aren't as fortunate.

This reminds me of one of my first interviews with Claudia. She told me she saw herself as "lucky." "No sé porque, pero siempre me toca suerte," she said. Claudia told me about a time when she found a hundred-dollar bill on the floor, "just like that, no más así." She bent over to pick it up thinking it was a dollar and was shocked that it was way more. We laughed. I told her my mom always said the same thing. She was always finding random change on the ground and had, a couple of times, also come across the rare large bill. She swore that it was because she was lucky and respected her luck by listening to it. "When you see a coin on the ground, you have to pick it up so that you will find more," my mom counseled. Something about how if you ignore the coin, your luck will go away, and you won't find any more money. She's proud to say she always picks up the coin and that's why her luck continues. Claudia completely agreed, adding that she, too, always picks up the coin.

Despite the many barriers and unreliable access to care, pain forced Claudia into the clinic, and because of that, someone detected the cancer cells. If my mom hadn't nearly fainted in Mexico and been forced to see another doctor, she might not be here today. Today my mom doesn't have to worry about cervical cancer, but given the numbers, she ran the risk too. Having your entire uterus removed, however, is not a preventative measure anyone wants to be forced to take. Still, if these women had had health insurance and regular access to good doctors, they would have been spared a lot of pain and suffering; they would have been treated before things got so bad—before fainting in public or suddenly being unable to move. It didn't have to be that way.

Cancers, tumors, malignant growths in the body, in the uterus. If, as many women feel, la matriz is the source of womanhood and motherhood, but it keeps getting attacked by cancer, what does that say about the traumas that Latinas, mexicanas, carry— the struggles and sustos that send our life-giving source into bloody shock? I wonder how many undocumented and uninsured Latinas are living with uterine diseases. How many are living with undiagnosed cervical cancer? How many will die from untreated cervical cancer, bleed out from a random hemorrhage, or have an unexpected heart attack from undiagnosed anemia? How many undocumented and uninsured Latinas will get preventable cervical cancer because they don't have regular, humane access to health care? A simple search on the internet responds dispassionately to my question in the first dozen headlines: "Hispanic Women Less Likely to Survive Endometrial Uterine Cancer," "The Crisis of Cervical Cancer among Latinas." Medical reports shouting death sentences in bold, uppercase titles.[1]

I asked Claudia how she felt about her medical exclusion and the limited access for her and her daughter. I asked her what she thought about the xenophobic discourse she heard in the media and all the negative things that were being said about immigrants.

"Mal. Muy mal," she responded. "And sometimes I get scared because in the first place, I never wanted to come over here. Never. Ever. Never was it in my plans to come here and be undocumented, illegal, or whatever they call us. But I do get scared because I see how much progress my girl has made here. So I worry more about her than anything else, right? She has progressed so much here. So much. So much. Her, more than anyone else. I know that here she can have una carrera chiquita, a little career. She can be an interpreter. She can maybe even be a teacher, or an assistant or something, right? So, well, here I see more of a future for her than in Mexico, where I lived and where there is nothing for her. So I do get scared. I get scared that the laws are changing and getting stricter, and they say that the police now are going to work with Immigration now that they approved SB4. All I can do is pray. If they were to catch me now, they would take me back to the detention center. Then they would give me a ten-year deportation. In other words, they increase the punishment. Once I have the ten-year deportation, if I were to come back into the US and get caught, then I could go to jail for up to a year. It's really complicated, pero pues sí, si me llegaran aventar, then I wouldn't come back. But if they ever take me, I want them to take me with my girls.

"So yes, I do get scared. I do. Because of all of that. But until now, in these years that I have been here, I have not been stopped for anything, not even a ticket. Nothing. I drive very well. I am very careful when I drive. I drive the limit and everything. These days I am more scared to leave the house. I wasn't as much before. But now, yes, I am. Before, I would go out to the stores, not to buy anything, right? But just to see. I would go out with my sisters-in-law in the street, driving back and forth. But now I don't go out at all. I don't go anywhere. I just go from the house to the school and from the school back to the house. Ever since the SB4 law went into effect. Because before I was out and about, out and about. But now with SB4—no, not anymore. I just stay here. Every day. At night when my husband gets home, then we go to the grocery store if we need to, but otherwise, we don't really go out."

Some time after our conversations together, I invited Claudia to a birthday party at my home. She had invited us to Nati's birthday previously, and I wanted to reciprocate the invitation. It took Claudia some time to respond, so I wasn't sure that she was going to come. When I saw her at school one day, she told me that she was waiting to hear from her comadre Beatriz to see if she was going too. At first, I thought maybe Claudia was just reluctant to come because she was worried that she wouldn't know anyone there. I had also invited Beatriz because her daughter was also a good friend of my son's. But Claudia wasn't feeling anxious about the party—that wasn't why she was waiting on Beatriz to respond first. It was because I live on the other side of town, about thirty minutes away, farther than Claudia and her family were comfortable driving unless it was absolutely necessary. But Beatriz is a permanent US resident, so if she would be going to the party, then she could drive them. It wouldn't feel as dangerous for Claudia and her daughters, and it would make her more comfortable. Although I also valued Beatriz's company, after that, any time I invited Claudia to my home, I made sure to also invite Beatriz. They were a package deal, their closeness marked by deep friendship and trust. This experience, however, highlighted for me the invasiveness of Claudia's undocumented status—how it seeped and spilled into every corner and crevice of her life.

How many times had I taken my children to birthday parties in any given month or year? Once, twice, five times, ten times? My mind would usually be preoccupied with all the things I had to do to prepare for the party: gifts, wrapping, bows, gift cards. Did I remember to RSVP and map the directions? But what I wasn't thinking about was, What if I get pulled over by a cop and deported while I'm driving to this party? What if they detain me, take my children, and I never see my family again? No, I've never had that fear while driving to a birthday party or anywhere, and chances are, unless you're undocumented, neither have you. For Claudia, this fear isn't just an anxious thought, a worst-case scenario drummed up in her brain; it's a very real possibility. Not only can it happen, it has happened many times to many families. Family separation is the new American slogan: "Give me your tired, your poor, your huddled masses yearning to breathe free . . . and we'll separate their families and disappear them into detention centers or across borders they may not know."

Thousands of mothers like Claudia are tormented by the thought of potentially driving to a birthday party or a doctor's appointment and never coming home. I thought back to other undocumented mothers I had spoken with. One thing that stood out in all of their stories was that they felt the most afraid when they were traveling somewhere. "Es en el camino," they emphasized almost in unison. It was in the trip from one place to another that these women felt the most fear, in the obscure, in-between spaces of travel, in the journey. And SB4 had only intensified that fear. For Claudia, every excursion outside her home, even to the store, was a replay of her migration—with every trip bringing back memories of the border and the fear of having to face it again. Later I found out that Claudia and her husband had already had a very close call.

"I remember in the beginning, when I first got here, I was scared all the time. Here we see a lot of airplanes and helicopters, and every time one would pass, I would say, 'They're going to see me, they're going to see me!' I was traumatized. I would see a police car and tún tún tún tún tún tún, mi corazón. I would tell my husband, 'What if they come? What if they find me?' He would tell me not to worry. He would say, 'You're here now. You're here now. You're safe here.' One day a police officer stopped us because they said my husband didn't do the stop right. Dios mío. Mi corazón. I wanted to jump out of the car and take off running. But I didn't because I thought, My daughters are in the car. Well, they just gave us a ticket and told my husband he needs to be careful with the stops and do them right. They gave him a ticket and that was all. I was so relieved. But I tell you that I was thinking the whole time, How do I run and how do I take my daughters? When it was over, my husband just said, 'Ya ves, Chaparra, no pasa nada. No. No, pasa nada.' I think now, Wow, I was out of my mind back then. It would hit me like that, but now, well, I'm used to it. I know we were lucky. The police officer was buena gente, and he just gave us a ticket. That was our first time ever being stopped in all these years, and it hasn't happened again, but I'm terrified that we might be stopped again, and we won't be as lucky. So, just here. I just stay here, close to my house. I don't go far, never. The truth is I really don't go anywhere anymore. I spend all day at home. The time passes, twelve o'clock, one, the day ends, and here I am. Sometimes in the afternoon I go to Zumba, to do some exercise, because, you know, but that's all. Then I go and pick up Nati from school and I come back home."

I paused to thank Claudia for sharing her life story with me. We weren't done talking, but something about hearing her illness narrative and seeing exactly how the trauma from her migration had manifested itself in her body—making itself known as physical pain, tumors, and daily spiritual and psychological torment—reminded me to recognize how difficult these conversations might be for her. "I know it's not a simple thing to ask you to take time out of your day to relive all of these memories," I said. "I know how busy you are as a mother and everything you have to take care of."

"Yes, we women are the pillars of our homes, and we have to be attentive to everything," Claudia responded. "And sometimes we don't even realize how much we do because we're just so used to doing it all. Each day that passes we do it over again, and we survive that way, day after day. Every day we thank God for getting us through one more day. Every day we give thanks, y es así."

We went on to talk about how as mothers and women we especially carry so much of the emotional labor of our homes, for our children but also for our husbands. "My husband is so sensitive," Claudia interjected, "but he's not good at communicating. Recently, not too long ago, his nephew died crossing the border. He was on his way over here to live with us. He died in the mountains. It happened recently, when the snow came down, that's when he died. That's why the crossings are so dangerous. My husband has been so sad since that happened. He has cried, and cried, and cried since we heard. His nephew was only nineteen. So I tell my husband, 'Let it all out. Just let it out. Cry! But talk to me. Talk to me!' Because he suffers from seizures, and I didn't want all that to stay atacado, bottled up, and then cause an attack. So I would say, 'Please talk to me. Desahógate.' But he wouldn't. I kept insisting until one day, he finally started to talk to me, and he talked and talked. He let it all out. I was so relieved because his attacks are bad, feos.

"He gets, um, stiff. He falls stiff, and he's a big guy, so nobody can move him, or fold him, or anything. He's also allergic to penicillin. One time the doctors gave him an injection of penicillin, and he got very fat, very swollen. His eyes closed up. But, well, it's been a long time since he had an attack. He says he knows exactly when an attack is going to hit him. He knows right away. He says he gets a terrible headache and his heart races, tún tún tún tún tún. He was taking a really strong medication for the seizures. My family even thought that maybe that was why it happened, because the medication is in his body, right? That maybe all that medication passed into me and that was what provoked Nati's condition. That maybe the medication was too strong for her. I asked the doctors and they said no, that they didn't see any evidence of that. They told me that has nothing to do with it. But who knows?

"His medication is also very expensive now. So he stopped taking it because it's expensive, but also because he hates taking medication. I tell you, he's worse than my daughters. He doesn't want to take the medication. He doesn't want to go to the doctor. He gets angry and says, 'I don't want to go.' I say, 'Papi, let's go.' I fight with him to get his general checkup. I like to do the general checkup because that's how I found out I was very sick. But with my husband it's hard. I worry because he's big and overweight. Even though they never find anything in him. He doesn't have cholesterol, he doesn't have triglycerides, he doesn't have anything. He's healthier than all of his brothers. They do have cholesterol. All of his brothers are all big like him, but some are very skinny. He is the only one that came out healthy, just him out of all of them. He just has that, the seizures.

"I remember when we were dating in Mexico. He would get really sick all the time. The medications were really expensive, even over there. It doesn't happen as often anymore. Every now and then. One time he was at work and it hit him. It was back when I was still in Mexico. He didn't want to scare me, so he didn't tell me until years later. I get so scared that it will hit him again because he works with heavy machinery. He works a lot on those big machines. They tell me that the time it hit him, he was getting off one of the machines, and he fell and hit the wheel so hard he had wheel marks on his body. That's how hard he hit the wheel. The good thing is people saw him and helped him. So I do worry about him, a lot. It doesn't happen often anymore. Now it only happens when he gets angry. Just when he gets angry. When he gets angry or when something makes him feel bad and bad and bad, that's when he feels it, y de coraje, de coraje, his mouth turns purple and one single tear will come out of his eye, but a very thick tear, thick, thick, and then, right away, we know it's going to hit."

Claudia spoke about her husband's seizures and medical history in detail and with deep concern for his safety. When she talked about how his body would just fall stiff, and no one could help him because he was so big, she would pause and take a deep breath. It was clear that this, too, caused Claudia much distress. "He's worse than my daughters," she lamented. It was one thing to take a child to the doctor, but it was another entirely to convince an adult and fellow parent and partner that he needed to care for his health.

Claudia didn't always have time to stop and take care of her own physical pain because she was busy taking care of everyone else. Her occasional neglect for her body was because of the struggle of having very little time and support to care for herself, a struggle compounded by barriers that made every effort to seek medical help much more difficult than it needed to be. The same was partially true for her husband. Throughout her story, Claudia emphasized that her husband worked long hours and rarely had time to see them, let alone accompany her to the doctor or take himself to the doctor. The difference is that Claudia's husband had Claudia.

"I take care of him. I pack him a good lunch. I make sure he eats right, and even if he gets mad, I tell him to go to the doctor. I worry about him so much because he's so sensitive. But then it's not always that way for me. One time when my mom was bitten by a dog in Mexico, and I was so worried about her, I would call him at work to talk because I was worried, and he would just say, 'Oh, okay. Well, okay. Ándale, I'm busy. I need to go back to work.'

"'¡Válgame, Dios!' I would say. 'I need you to tell me something too!' Sometimes I tell him that I feel so lonely, and you know what he says? He tells me to go clean! ¡Qué feo!" Claudia chuckled, just as her baby came barging into the living room.

4 | COMADRES

"THERE'S ONLY HER." CLAUDIA SMILED. "MORE THAN anyone, it's her. She's my comadre. Fíjate que la conocí no más de vista. You know, I saw Beatriz and I knew we were going to be friends. I met her at the preschool, Nati's first school. She used to always drive up in a truck, or I would see her walk up with her daughter and her son. That was when he was alive, may God bless him. One day I just walked with her and started talking to her and that's how it started, just like that, no más así. Then when we had to meet with the school, because they were going to close and pass us on to another school, she asked me where I was going to take Nati and I just said, 'The truth is, I don't know. Wherever the district sends me. I'll just let them choose.' Later, she asked me again, and I said the same thing, but she said, 'Hold on. Let's find out together.'

"She helped me ask about the school and whether they would wear a uniform or not because I didn't know. So the girls ended up at the same school and in the same class, and that's when we really became close. Whenever there were meetings, Beatriz would translate for me. She would tell me to ask the teacher questions. She would say, 'Ask her this and ask her that.' I call her all the time about homework to check what it means. I will say, 'Beatriz, the homework says they have to take this or that,' and she will explain it to me. Sometimes she would call me to ask what time I was leaving the house to pick Nati up from school, and she'd say, 'Leave earlier so we can talk!' So I always go earlier so we can spend a little while echando chisme, just talking about life. I'll tell her about my struggles with Nati's teachers, and she would give me advice. Back then she would always tell me to

talk to the teacher and to take a little notebook to write down
my questions and what she said. She always told me to stand up
for myself and Nati. She gives me a lot of advice and support.
Even when I was trying to buy hearing aids for Nati, she supported me a lot."

When Claudia and I initially met, she asked me if I wanted
to join a raffle for a faux designer bag. "It's only five dollars," she
said. "I'm going use the money to buy a new hearing aid for my
daughter." She explained that Nati kept breaking her hearing
aids, and this time they had to be replaced. I wondered if five
dollars per person would be enough, but Claudia told me that
she was asking all the mothers at Nati's school and that Beatriz

was also helping her recruit people. I agreed to join, and Claudia handed me a red ticket. I had been a part of many raffles before but never for a child's hearing aid. Vividly aware of the limits of the health care system, Claudia didn't waste any time taking matters into her own hands. She was there that day with a roll of raffle tickets and the purse to model. She was ready and prepared to recruit people to help her daughter. Claudia explained that raffles were common in her community. People participated because it was affordable and because they would need the help one day too. The raffle itself represents lives that are fundamentally grounded in community, where resources are often shared and where families and neighbors engage each other to improve their conditions together. For undocumented mothers, being connected to other women and families in their communities is essential to their ability to advocate for themselves and their children, especially since many women leave their own community of mothers when they migrate. Some time after this meeting, I ran into Beatriz. I had completely forgotten about the raffle, but when I saw her, I remembered. "I guess I didn't win," I called out from across the school lawn. She laughed. "¡N'ombre! María won!" "Qué bueno," I said. It made me happy to see how invested Beatriz was in the whole thing. I was glad that Claudia had raised the money she needed for Nati, and that she had a friend like Beatriz who provided that kind of support.

"So she has become a true friend," Claudia continued. "Una comadre, pues, and like I told you, our friendship is unconditional. For better or for worse, she is always there. I tell her, '¡Beatriz, nunca vayamos a salir mal tú y yo!' And she says, 'Never! Even if the girls stop talking and become enemies, not us, no. We will always stay friends. Let them figure it out, but we will always be together.' And now that our daughters are in different classrooms, it's still the same between us. I still call her all the time, like 'Beatriz, are they going to wear costumes?' or 'Beatriz, what about this other thing?' And she still says, 'Come on, let's do this together. Come over to my house and we can work on these projects together. You do yours and I'll do mine, but here together.' 'Okay, that's good,' I say. And that's how it is between us. We do everything together. Here and there, andamos allí las dos.

"She helps me a lot at school, but it's more than that. If I say, 'Beatriz, llévanos al Texas Children's,' she will do it. She has taken us to the doctor many times. Or she will check on me when we have appointments. She will say, 'Clau, are you guys at the doctor?' or 'Clau, se te hace tarde para ir al doctor. Tienes cita.' 'No, sí, yo lo sé,' I say. Beatriz is the one person that is more involved with the doctors. More than anyone, except my husband, right? How do I explain? She is the one that is más al pendiente de eso, pues. She makes sure I don't forget an appointment, or she will ask me questions like do I know if there will be a translator for me or if someone will be able to help me with the baby when I take Nati. I often say that Beatriz's cariño for Nati is sincere, and for me too, right? Her love for me is also sincere. Because you know, she also suffered a lot with her son. I think for that reason too, right? She . . . it's like she must think, Well, I didn't like it when people made fun of my son or stared at him or treated him like less. She tells me, 'You don't allow it either, Clau. You go to the office, you go there, you tell the doctor what you need to tell them. Don't let anyone silence you or deny you.'

"Me regañaba también. She would get on my case about taking notes! She says, 'Apúntale, you always write it down. Take a notebook with you and write down everything you want to ask the doctor and write down what the doctor says!' That is her thing. She's always reminding me to take notes and ask questions. Then when I see her, she always asks me how the appointments went. She will say, 'How did it go with the doctor?' I say, 'Well, it went like this or that.' And she will say, 'And did you ask him about that?' If I say, 'No, I forgot,' then she gets upset with me and says, 'Es qué that's why I told you to write it down in a notebook!' So it's like that with her, and that's how we are. Sometimes she asks me more questions than the doctor! She is always thinking about Nati. She helps me a lot with her. Sometimes she will say, 'Clau, take Nati to this other doctor, he's very good.' Or she will recommend a good clinic or a good hospital. Or she will tell me to go and ask and find more information. I will say, 'Yes, I went, and they sent me here or there.' I keep her updated."

Claudia looked happy when she spoke about Beatriz, and there was light in her eyes, which said even more than her words.

It was clear that Beatriz was special to Claudia because she cared about her, and worried about her, and was there for her, "in good times and bad." Claudia spoke about Beatriz as if she were speaking of a marriage partner, a wife. She said her relationship with Beatriz was unconditional. That is the meaning of comadrazgo—unconditional love, trust, and support, for better or for worse, in the good times and the bad. It's a kind of unconditional love and understanding that only comadres can give each other because it comes from a situated knowledge: of knowing what it feels like to be a woman, a mother, to be Mexican, to be treated differently, to have a child with a disability, to carry the weight of everything, to feel the struggle deep in the skin.

So much life happens in the day to day of mothering. Most of it is undocumented, barely acknowledged, rarely verbalized, just lived. So much life also happens in the many years it takes to write a book. Writing Claudia's story over the past several years has meant there have also been major changes in my life, as mother, daughter, and granddaughter. In the middle of a raging global pandemic in 2020, my abuelita died. Her name is Maria Luisa Farfán, que en paz descanse. Her comadres called her Luisa. I call her Abuelita.

Because of the pandemic, I wasn't able to spend the last months of her life with her. I was forced to see her only briefly on the screen of my phone, trying desperately to fit in as much conversation and "contact" as I could before she grew tired. In the last few months, it was harder for her to stay on the phone—our long and passionate conversations slowly, but notably, shortening over time. When I started this book, I knew that I wanted to interview my mother and grandmother because they both raised me. I don't know how to describe how hard it is to sit down with the busy, exhausted women that made you and ask them about their lives. It's not easy—at least it wasn't for me—so it took time for me to do it. But I thought I would have more time with my grandmother.

Comadres are not always chosen; sometimes they're gifted mothers, mothers we never had who are put in our lives to guide us. My grandmother was that person for my mother, who was only seventeen when she became a mother. My mom loves to say that she had a deeper relationship with my grandmother than my grandmother had with any of her seven daughters. Having watched them for most of my life—the way they interacted, took care of each other, enjoyed each other, but also traded passive-aggressive responses and lovingly annoyed glances—I believed her. I'm positive my mom wouldn't call my grandmother a comadre, because she just saw her as a mother, but I still think that their co-mothering relationship was special and more than just a daughter- and mother-in-law relationship. My grandmother mothered me and my brother, and in the process mothered my mother. She took the responsibility of caring for my brother and me when my parents needed to work, and still worked alongside my mother, helping her and my dad work to make ends meet. She held the reins of two families, all the while trying to walk her own life. When my mom tells stories of how she became the woman that she is today, she often speaks of my grandmother Luisa.

Before my abuelita grew so weak she could no longer stay awake, a transition that felt like a blink, I got to see her in person. I wore two masks and sat with her in the garden, a situation that bothered my grandmother so very much. "Ay, hija," she said over and over. "Qué pena que no te puedo dar un agua, algo de comer." It troubled her so much that she couldn't feed me and care for me like she wanted to in that moment. It also made me incredibly uncomfortable to refuse her hospitality. It felt disrespectful and, most of all, cruel.

I saw her, and in that garden, emotionally frayed from the pandemic and worried about her health, I finally asked her the question I'd always wanted to ask: "How did you do it, Abuelita?" How did you raise nine children and thirteen grandchildren across two borders with little support and sometimes barely enough to eat?"

"Hija, no era fácil," she sighed. "Eran muchos muchachos. Pero yo decía, bueno, así es. Sí, uno se estresa y se enoja. ¿Cómo no, verdad? Así es la vida. Así es. Pero no se me olvida lo que me dijo una de mis comadres. Un día me vio, digo, yo creo me vio muy mal. No sé, pero me dijo, 'Luisa, lo único que no puedes hacer es quedarte con nada adentro. No te quedes con nada adentro. Desahógate. Como sea, pero hazlo. Porque así, agarrándonos de corajes o estrés, así es como se enferma uno.' Y tenía mucha razón. Entonces haz lo que tengas que hacer, hija. Toma tu tiempo. Pero no te quedes con nada adentro."

My abuelita's comadre had reminded her how dangerous it is to keep things bottled up, to hold on to anger and stress in the body. She didn't know if, or how, her comadre had read the pain in her expression on that day since my grandmother, like my mother, usually had a strong poker face. She was an expert at looking like everything was perfectly fine and under total control. It's actually one of the things I most admired about her: her apparent resoluteness and perpetually unbothered demeanor. It's what I saw, anyhow, through the eyes of an adoring granddaughter who still has a hard time believing her grandmother was a mere human—humanity feeling much too *basic* for my abuelita's grandeur. But she was human, and the struggles of motherhood and, well, life weighed on her too.

So many thoughts flooded me at once as I listened to my grandmother share her wisdom. I thought about myself, of course, of all the ways I did or did not un-drown myself on a daily basis. I thought about her health and how she had lived with diabetes for more than forty years without any serious complications because she took such meticulous care of herself. I also thought about how I'd always heard my mom, tías, and dad arguing over how my grandmother needed to relax more, and how all the kids needed to stop stressing her out because her emotions were so intricately interwoven with her health—her sugar and blood pressure responding to her fear and frustration like electricity responds to water. I reflected on how, despite what she was telling me about her comadre's advice, I had never once in my entire life heard my grandmother yell, in anger or frustration or reproach—never. Always poised and serene, never angry, at least not at me, her eyes could slice the world in half, but she always seemed cool. I know that isn't the version of her my tías and dad grew up with, but that's their story. My story is the version of my abuelita who recalled the words of her comadre and tried to live them out as best she could. I understood the message, and I received it from her comadre, from my abuelita to me.

As difficult as sending us across the border into the care of my abuelita was for my mother at the time, it was a gift to me. My mother's sacrifice was the beginning of my life in my grandmother's mentorship—a mentorship that would grant me unconditional belonging and teach me how to heal myself a hundred times over. My abuelita was like that—a healer and a mentor. Perhaps comadrazgo is also a form of mentorship, one born of experiences passed down as critical lessons between women who see each other through a lens of care and concern.

"Is there anyone else besides Beatriz that supports you like that? That you call 'comadre'?" I asked Claudia.

"Look, out of everyone, it's mostly Beatriz, but there is one other person." Claudia gestured with her hand, holding up one finger to her face to emphasize that there aren't many, but just one other person. "It's my brother-in-law's wife, Margarita. She is the only other person that has supported me a little more. We used to live with them when we first arrived. But that didn't work out. We disagreed a lot, mostly over the kitchen because we both wanted to cook for our families, and, well, there was only one stove. So we always came out disagreeing. But then we moved out, and that's when we developed a beautiful relationship.

"Sometimes when I'm sad, she'll call me and ask me how I'm doing. I'll tell her I'm feeling depressed and lonely, and she'll talk me through it. She'll say, 'No, Claudia, you need to fight it!' Or I'll say, 'Ay, Margarita, I got really sick,' and she'll sit and listen to everything I'm feeling. She was the one that was fussing with me and fussing with me to go to the doctor. Just these last three weeks I got really sick, and she was there saying, 'Go to the doctor, go to the doctor, go to the doctor.' If it wasn't for Margarita, I probably would've kept putting it off. She will even say, 'If you need me to watch the girls, just tell me.' She sometimes watches them for me if I need to go somewhere like that. But it's, oh, maybe once a year. It's very rare when she watches them because I don't ever go anywhere, and, well, she also studies, so she can't always do it. But she does support me a lot. I don't know how you say it. Is it emotional support? I don't know, but that's what she gives me. Así pues, me da aliento, ¿verdad?

"She supports me in that way. She gives me advice, and even when I get into arguments with my husband, she's the one I talk to. She's the only one I tell—well, except Beatriz—but only those two. They're the only ones with whom I share my intimate things, that I talk to about what happens with my husband or things like that. And they give me advice por un lado y por otro, tanto Beatriz como ella. Up until now, she has been a good sister-in-law and friend, and the same with Beatriz. Both have been my support, and both help me a lot with my girls. Me echan ánimo. They give me spirit. They tell me, 'Don't give up. No te dejes. Don't let anyone push you around. You have to keep going—tienes que echarle ganas—for your kids.' They remind me. They say, 'Because if you get sick, then who is going to take care of your daughters?' For everything they remind me about my girls, that I have to keep fighting for them, that I have to be strong and healthy for them. They are both very special."

While mothers are busy taking care of everyone else, who takes care of them? It was clear from Claudia's story, as it was in my mother's and my grandmother's, that comadres, other mothers, take care of mothers. Claudia depended on her comadres even to convince her to go to the doctor. They were the ones that looked out for her when she didn't look out for herself. Claudia's reflection on the everyday support and concern of her comadres could be that of so many women.

I thought back to a conversation with one of my tías. It was several years ago. We were visiting my grandmother, and because I hadn't seen my aunt in a long time, she wanted to know everything I was up to. At the time I was just beginning my research, and I told her a little about what I was finding—how the Affordable Care Act wasn't helping undocumented women, and how folks were really struggling to access quality health care, especially when it came to long-term, chronic illnesses. My aunt agreed that it was sad and unfortunate, but then quickly changed direction and, in what felt like a personal reprimand, said, "Pero nuestra gente también no se cuida." She went on. "Can you believe so many of us, we first have to go and ask our comadres before we go to the doctor? ¡Es que, por favor, señoras! You don't need permission to go to the doctor. If something hurts, if something feels wrong, we need to take care of ourselves! ¡Que comadre ni que nada! We should care for ourselves the way we take care of our kids. Why don't we do that? That's our problem."

This tía, the sixth-born of the nine and known for her unwavering personality, was infamous in the family for her limited patience and short fuse. I had learned early on to just nod when she said things full of conviction. Disagreeing with her usually led to a *very* long and stern lesson, and a reminder that I was "too young" to understand such "real-life" things. It wasn't the first time I would hear a similar lesson, or regaño, from her though. Years later, just days after my grandmother's passing, she would sit me down and, as though my life depended on it, tell me to take care of my health above all else. "Your kids will understand, hija, if you need to take time to yourself, and even if they don't, it doesn't matter. Usted se me cuida primero, ¿me entiende?" She used the formal *usted* to accentuate her seriousness, her eyes intently locked on mine.

Being raised by nine strong-willed mexicanas breeds a special kind of strength in you. When I was younger, I was terrified of this aunt, but as an adult and mother, I understood her better, and we had grown very close. She wasn't the youngest in the family, but she had enough older sisters and had seen enough of my grandmother's life to know the kind of invisible emotional and physical pain that mothers suffer in the world. She herself had recently been shocked by an early diagnosis of diabetes, one that sent her into a radically new lifestyle almost overnight. My tía's advice about taking care of myself above all else was stern and unyielding, but it came from her own deep regret— regret she felt for neglecting herself over the years, regret passed down from my grandmother, who would carry the weight of worry for her adult children into the afterlife. Despite what she said about comadres as health confidants, however, I had seen my tía consult her own comadres many times. Her comment didn't come from disdain but rather out of a real concern for the generational karma among women in our family—one that has left us repeating a story of prioritizing care for others over care for ourselves.

In my conversations with some health care providers and public health workers, there was often a collective disdain for the indirect and community-based ways in which Latinx communities tend to their health needs. This was expressed as frustration at what some folks called a "delay" in seeking care. Whether it was because some Latinas consulted their comadres, elders, or religious leaders before seeking medical care, the medical community seemed perplexed and impatient with this community-based process. This disdain for a more holistic and collective understanding of healing practices is born partly out of the arrogance of biomedicine, which sees itself as the only legitimate authority on healing, a conviction born out of Enlightenment-era rhetoric that couldn't be farther from the truth. But this intolerance is also born of a racist, classist, and paternalistic history of health care that has constructed working-class and poor communities of color as "primitive" and "backward" because of the way some center the collective over the individual and combine community and generational knowledge with scientific evidence.

One of the greatest deceptions of biomedicine is that health and illness are individual experiences. In fact, we know that these are social—that everything around us affects our physical health and that, in turn, when we get sick, it impacts everyone around us. Therefore, it only makes sense that healing is necessarily collective, and that having comadres to remind us to care for our own health amid so many other priorities could be an important part of staying healthy. I mean, how often do doctors themselves need to be reminded to take better care of their own health? For immigrant women like Claudia, who left her entire community of women behind in Mexico the day she decided to migrate, having local comadres in the United States who understand aspects of the system that they might not and who also understand their Mexican and migrant experience can be crucial to their survival. For many immigrant women, comadres are also health guardians, health advocates, and system mediators.

"Do you get to see Beatriz often?" I asked Claudia. "Not since she had the baby," she said. "Now that she's recovering from that, I don't see her as much because she doesn't come to the school. Before she had the baby, I would go to her house often, or if it was a Friday, she would come over to my house. She comes over and she says, 'Make me some pork legs! Okay?' She loves pork legs. So I will make her some spicy pork taquitos. Se los come bien sabroso because I make them with handmade tortillas! So she's always, 'Clau, make me the pork!' and I'm like, 'Ah, okay!' And that's how it is! But we are always together. She's at my house or I'm at her house. When she was pregnant, I would visit her a lot to check on her, but just for a little while, you know, because I don't like to be enfadosa. So just a little while here and there so that she can rest if she needs to. We used to always meet after school. We would go to McDonald's so that the girls could eat and play and do things like that, and we would talk for hours.

"She would tell me if she was worried about her pregnancy. Sometimes she would tell me she was up all night worried about the pregnancy. I usually knew about her appointments too. I tried to help in any way I could. So she will call and say, 'Okay, I'm about to get in the shower. Clau, can you come get the girls? Because I won't make it on time. I need to get ready fast to get to my appointment at seven.' So I run and I go pick up the girls, and I take them to school. Yo voy y le echo la mano porque a mí también me ha echado mucho la mano. So what does it matter if I need to leave five minutes earlier, or if I have to go there first, then to school or back home? It's what we do for each other. When she gets back from her appointment, I ask her, 'How was your ultrasound?' She tells me the baby is like this and needs this, and they increased my insulin, and little things like that. There was one appointment where I had to remind her, '¡Te toca cita!' And she said, 'Yes, I know, I'm on my way, but I'm so frustrated . . .' just complaining about this and that, you know? And then she called me later, really mad, to tell me that she changed that doctor because she didn't like her because she was too cold, and she didn't like how she was treating her. And then I said, 'Well, you have to tell her how you feel!' She responded, 'I do tell her! You know I don't care. You know I tell them what I think.' And I said, 'No, I know you do.' She didn't like that doctor because she said she didn't listen to her. Siempre la regañaba, decía. The doctor was always getting on her about this or that. But more than anything she didn't like the way the doctor treated her."

Claudia explained that Beatriz often felt that her doctor was condescending and treated her almost like a disobedient child rather than a veteran mother of three. Beatriz was dealing with prenatal diabetes for the first time in four pregnancies, but she was also nervous and particularly sensitive because she was having a boy. Her firstborn, also a boy, had a genetic disorder that ended his life when he was only nine years old. Even though years had passed since her son's death, and Beatriz had had two healthy pregnancies after that, having a boy again brought back all the painful memories and fear from those years. Prenatal diabetes is not uncommon and can usually be managed as long as the mother is going to regular prenatal visits. But any deviation from a "normal," healthy pregnancy can be stressful, especially if the mother has already had problems in the past. According to Claudia, the doctor regularly reprimanded Beatriz for her weight. Hyperaware of her own medical history, Beatriz was trying her best to stay healthy and active, but it wasn't easy, and feeling like the doctor was always disappointed with her, or indifferent, was really getting to her.

"'Ya no aguanto, Clau,' she would say when she started getting closer to her delivery date. 'Clau!' She would call me, desesperada. 'I can't take this anymore.' And I would say, 'Okay, come on, let's go for a walk.' We would go for walks, very slow, because ever since she got pregnant, it was complicated for her. So we would go on walks around two in the afternoon before picking up the kids at school. We would walk for almost forty-five minutes going around the school. 'Wait, wait, wait, I'm feeling pressure down here,' she would say, and I would get on her case because the doctor told her to wear a faja. But she would complain that 'la faja me cala' and that it was uncomfortable and that she had to take it off to shower, and 'Okay, then,' I would say. Step by step we would go like that. Oh, the thing that was so funny, and I would make fun of her, is that she couldn't be not even five minutes without having to use the bathroom—the bathroom, to the bathroom, five minutes, ten minutes and to the bathroom. Five minutes and 'Let's go to the school office to use the bathroom!' We were in that office two, three times a day! 'Beatriz,' I would say, 'I'm going to buy you a diaper! One of those from Walmart. They say they are very comfortable!' One time . . . Wait, don't put this part in your book, okay?

"Pero son muchas cosas divertidas que paso con ella. We have so much fun together. She's a really good friend. For everything she cusses too. It makes me laugh because it's not aggressive stuff, you know? It's not like that. It's different. It's like, ella tiene la maña to speak like that . . . to just say 'chinga tu madre.' Está bien loca. I tell her, 'Beatriz, ya no me la mientes tanto because I really miss my mom.' And she says, 'Pero yo te la miento para que te acuerdes de ella.' And we laugh so hard, and I say, '¡Ay, qué mala eres! I talk to my mom every day.' Really, not even one day goes by that I don't talk with my mom early in the morning—not one day. And Beatriz says, 'Well, so that you can think of her even more!' I say, 'No, es que se siente feo,' and she says, 'Ay, chinga tu madre.' Me hace reír. That's one thing I love about her. Oh, and she gets on my case too. Me regaña. She gets on me about school and makes sure that I'm keeping up with what the girls need to do, and that I'm asking questions and getting help. She says, 'Clau, the girls have to do this all week, are you doing it?' or 'Clau, how are you going to dress the girls tomorrow?' or 'Clau, there's a project,' or 'Clau, the girls need to do this or that.' She checks on me, you know, to make sure I know what's going on because sometimes I don't know, or sometimes I don't understand what the teachers want, so Beatriz makes sure so that the girls don't miss out.

"Just one time, sí, salimos mal. Just one time she got mad at me for real. I didn't remember, or no me había fijado, that the girls were supposed to wear red and blue to school, I think . . . I don't remember. Or red and white. And she called me and said, 'Clau, did you dress Nati?' I hadn't remembered, so I said, 'Oh, no! Did they have to dress up? I didn't know.' She said, 'Chinga tu madre, tú nunca te pones las pilas. Nunca sabes lo que está pasando en la escuela . . .' And I got upset because that's not true. I told her, 'Beatriz, siempre estoy al pendiente del escuela, con los papeles que les mandan, but I forgot about this. I just forgot, and honestly, no one called me to tell me.' I didn't know. Really, no one called me to tell me that they had to dress up. It wasn't until that day that they called me, and so that was the day she got mad at me. And she said that I never know anything, and I told her, 'It's that you get mad over nothing,' and she said that it was my fault, that I wasn't paying attention. And no, that's not true, siempre estoy al pendiente de las niñas. I just forgot this one thing. So yes, that time we did get mad with each other y salimos mal for a little while, but up until now, that's the only time ever."

All friendships have their ups and downs. Friends fight, often with as much passion as they love. Comadres are friends, but they're also co-mothers, and that means there are all the layers of both kinds of relationships—of friends looking out for each other and of mothers wanting to care for each other as they would care for their own children. For various reasons, I didn't get a chance to formally interview Beatriz, but I did speak with her occasionally at school and was able to see her and Claudia together on many occasions—at drop-off and pickup, PTA meetings, school events, and sometimes at birthdays and baby showers. It was clear that Beatriz cared for Claudia in more ways than one. Beatriz thought about Claudia's and her daughters' needs often, almost out of habit, as if they were her own children.

I saw how Claudia and Beatriz took turns picking each other's children up from school—something that was not only an indication of their mutual trust, but that also required that they officially list each other as trusted guardians with the school. They were family. But even though Beatriz loved Claudia and sometimes felt frustrated out of sincere concern, there were aspects of Claudia's life that even she couldn't fully understand. It upset Claudia that Beatriz could be so hard on her the day she forgot to dress Nati for the special school event, but she forgave her because she understood that, deep down, it came out of love. Their argument, however—especially the intensity of Beatriz's frustration over Claudia's "not knowing" about a school event—illustrates the deep and all-encompassing struggle of being an undocumented mother, a struggle with many arms that reach far and touch entire communities.

Claudia told me that Beatriz had requested to become an even more formal godmother to her children. Painfully aware of her friend's vulnerable immigration status, Beatriz offered to sign a power of attorney that would give her the right to make decisions—most importantly, medical and educational decisions—for Claudia's daughters in the event that she and her husband were ever deported. "She told me, 'Déjame a las niñas. I will take care of them and take them to visit you every year. No, every six months.'" The idea of signing over her parental rights to her comadre forced Claudia to imagine the unimaginable, a future for her daughters even if it would be without her. It was like planning for her death, except she wasn't dying. This was a very difficult topic for Claudia. Even as she tried to explain that Beatriz was acting out of love, she could barely speak past the tears and the imagined pain of leaving her daughters, especially Nati. I wanted to ask for clarification, like what brought this issue up. It seemed to come out of nowhere, on one of those random days when Claudia invited Beatriz over for pork legs. But perhaps it was something Beatriz had been thinking about for a while? Perhaps it was a concern that was intensified by SB4 and the increased attacks on undocumented communities? I didn't ask any more questions because I could tell it was very painful to remember.

After a few minutes though, Claudia regained her voice and adamantly proclaimed, "No, yo le dije gracias, but that I would never do that. If I were to be deported, I would leave with my daughters. I would take them with me and start over in Mexico." "I understand," I responded.

It felt like we had reached a border in our conversation about comadrazgo, a boundary. I wasn't sure yet, but it forced me to pause. Comadres can also be godmothers. My first formal intro-duction to comadrazgo was through my mother's comadre, my madrina. A madrina, a godmother, is the woman who baptizes you before the Catholic Church, the mother chosen by your parents to care for you if anything were to happen to them. In other words, a madrina is a comadre to whom you would entrust your children's lives. I guess up until that point I imagined Beatriz was Nati's madrina, but that didn't seem to be the case—or it was different given Claudia's undocumented status. There aren't any manuals for how to be an undocumented mother; there's no parenting book with a chapter called "Ten Steps to Choosing a Deportation Madrina." Not to mention, it felt like Claudia had been caught off guard. She had been living as an undocumented mother for several years already, and clearly the possibility of being deported was never far from her mind, but being asked to consider giving her daughters up, just like that, on a regular Friday over pork legs, seemed too much for her to bear. Later Claudia would return to this episode on her own.

The conversations I had with Claudia about her comadres took up many pages of transcript, but in the end, she didn't have to say much because there was a deep understanding between us of how comadrazgo works. Claudia emphasized the emotional support and presence of her comadres, doing and saying things that helped her carry the physical and emotional load of life, but I understood that it was more than that, and that there weren't really words for the other parts. Words fall short in translating the depth of support, care, and concern that comadres have for each other. More than concern, it's really pendiente. *Estar al pendiente* means to be in a constant and active state of awareness and concern. Pendiente, pending, pender, or depending, depender. It's the kind of concern Mexican mothers describe in relation to our children, but it is also one that comadres have for each other.

"No one listens to us like our comadres," Claudia emphasized. "Not our husbands, not our children, and not our parents. No one ... I think the most important thing is that I trust Margarita and Beatriz. I have other family members, cuñadas, that have been here a long time, nineteen and almost twenty years, and when I have tried to go to them, open myself up to them, they went and told other people. I trusted them with very personal things, and they went spreading gossip. So I stopped because I thought, They are going to be out there gossiping about me and laughing at me and who knows what else. They also judge me, judge my decisions and my things, and well, that's not okay. But with Beatriz and Margarita, I can trust them. I can open up to them. They show concern for me, and many times they have told me, 'I'm here if you need me.' Beatriz will say, 'You can cry with me. You don't have to put it on Facebook or tell other people. If you want to get angry, or scream, you can call me and do that. You can scream at me and cry with me, that's okay.' They look out for me like that. Me dejan que me desahogue con ellas, and I know it's safe because they have never betrayed me, and I know they don't judge me.

"I mean, I can defend myself too. My mom taught me to not take anything from anyone, de gente así de la calle, que ni conoces, ¿verdad? Gente that want to judge me, or look down on me, or make me feel like I'm less than them. I don't allow that. That I learned from my mom. I didn't live with my mom because I lived with my abuelita. But she would always tell us, my mom would tell us when she visited us, she said, 'No se dejen pisotear por nadie.' It was good advice, but in a way not always good because, like I said, I know how to defend myself, and I can be very sensitive about some things. When it comes to defending myself and the people I love, soy una fiera."

Desahogarse, to un-drown oneself, is a common Mexican expression. Just as my grandmother and later my aunt had reminded me to un-drown myself often, to release anger, stress, and sorrow so that it doesn't stay bottled up inside, so too had Beatriz and Margarita reminded Claudia. They gave her a safe space to release emotion that might stay pent up or, worse, come out in places and with people that weren't safe. With all the things that Claudia was carrying—the debilitating pain of fibromyalgia, the pressure to find quality care for her daughter, the unrelenting school system, the violent scrutiny of immigrant policing, as well as everyday struggles of motherhood and marriage—she needed a safe place where she could let out everyday feelings. A space where she could complain, yell, cry, let out the fiera, the fury, if she needed to, or just laugh about it all.

I keep thinking about my abuelita saying, "Hija, desahógate, no te quedes con nada adentro." How she knew the damage that untended emotions could cause, the way trauma can wreak havoc on our physical, mental, and spiritual health. Fibromyalgia was a physical manifestation of Claudia's trauma, and she knew it could be intensified by stress. My grandmother's blood pressure would spike and her sugar would spin out when she was overly stressed, worried, or angry. Trauma had a way of making itself known and seen. Less visible, and undocumented, was the ocean of never-ending, and all-encompassing, pendiente that Claudia lived in as a woman, mother, and undocumented immigrant. Talking with her comadres was a way for Claudia to un-drown herself, to come up for air and breathe as deeply and profoundly as she needed to, without judgment.

5 | NATALIA

"AY, AMIGA, NO TE HE PLATICADO. LET ME GO BACK IN time a little bit. I forgot to tell you about that time Nati was at school and she caught a facial paralysis. It happened last year. Nati was five, so yes, it was last year. Y me molesté mucho con las maestras. I got really upset with her teachers, and I went and complained to the principal. Well, let me start from the beginning because even when I remember, I get angry all over again. That day I took her to school, in the morning she was complaining that her molar hurt. I thought, Well, her molar hurts, and even Beatriz asked, 'Why is Nati's mouth like that?' And I said, 'Because her molar hurts.'

"At that time, she had Miss M. as her teacher. Yes, it was Miss M. Well, when I picked her up from school later that day, I see her mouth is worse, and I say, 'Nati, come let me see your mouth.' When I got closer to examine her mouth, I took a good look at her, and I noticed that the entire side of her face, this side, was horrible—her eye was bad, her mouth all the way down here, the whole side of her face, pues, was fallen like it had melted. I got so scared and worried, and I said, 'Oh honey, what's wrong? Why is your face like this?' Well, in that moment the teacher, Miss M., came out and said, 'Oh yeah, I was going to ask you about that. I was going to ask you if something happened to Nati because her face is like that.' I just stared at her and said, 'This morning I bathed her and brushed her hair, and her face was not like this.' I said, 'And if you saw her like this at school, then you should have called me to tell me, to ask me if I knew her face was like this!'

"I was so mad, but I was more worried about Nati. I got in the car, and I immediately drove her to the hospital. At that time, I was lucky I had the Gold Card,[1] so I grabbed her and took her to LBJ Hospital.[2] I signed in and everything because there they will usually see you without an appointment, but I signed her in for an appointment. It was late. It was already four in the afternoon, and like always, there were a lot of people there. I just watched as my baby's face got worse and worse, and her mouth fell more and more. I got so scared that I couldn't wait anymore. I jumped up and told the receptionist that she was getting worse, and they had to take her in now! By an act of God, yes, they listened and took her right away to the emergency room. They checked her, and weighed her, and measured her blood pressure and everything. They left her a little while in observation and told me . . . they told me that if I hadn't taken her when I did, if I had waited longer, if I had waited until the next day, that her face could have stayed permanently deformed. The doctor told me that Nati's facial paralysis was probably provoked by a trauma to her head.

"I was so angry and scared. The day before it happened, Nati had hurt her ear at school. She came home with her ear really bruised, really purple, really purple, and her ear is on her head, right? That was another thing that happened that the teacher didn't tell me about. So I told the doctor that Nati had come home from school the day before with her ear wounded, that something hit her ear, right? I told the doctor, 'If you can assure me that this paralysis happened because of the trauma to her ear, that was also a trauma to her head, I can blame the school because they didn't tell me. They didn't let me know so that I could take her to the doctor to get checked or at least observe her and make sure she was okay.' But the doctor told me he couldn't, that they couldn't really certify that it was because of that trauma. He told me it was caused by a trauma, but he couldn't certify it was that trauma. But I said, 'Then what is it?' That's the only trauma she had, and it just happened the day before the paralysis! It was obvious to me that was the cause, but that was it, and there was nothing I could do because the doctor wouldn't certify it was the trauma to her ear. But still, I blamed the school. Even though the doctor said he really didn't know what caused the paralysis, I knew the truth.

"So yes, that time I did go, and I wrote it all down, and made a complaint against the teacher y luego me arranqué con la directora. I went to the principal, and I told her what the doctor told me—that Nati's facial paralysis was caused by a trauma to her head, and that if I had waited longer, her face could have been permanently damaged. I told her that Nati had come home from school the day before with a trauma to her ear, and I even took pictures of her ear to show her how it was really purple. I showed her pictures, dates, and everything, and I said, 'Look, here are the pictures!' I told her that at no point had anyone called me to tell me what happened. I told her that they should have said something, right away, as soon as they saw her like that, because that was something that needed immediate attention. They had to give her medication immediately.

"The principal got really scared because she saw that the trauma to her ear happened at the school and so did the facial paralysis. She told me that I should have come straight to her office from the beginning. I'm telling you, the principal got really scared. Well, from there the teacher stopped, um, she stopped talking to me and would make mean faces at me and ignore me. But I don't care, I was defending what is mine. I mean, she had no right. She had no right and I told you, remember, I told you that she treated me less than others. I don't want other people's things, right? But I think everyone should be treated equally. Sometimes Beatriz's daughter will miss school, and the teacher will call Beatriz directly. 'Is your daughter okay? Did something happen?' But if my daughter missed school, nothing. No calls. Nobody would call to check on her. I mean, I think it needs to be the same for every student, right? And in that moment, she should've called me. It was her responsibility to call me. To say, 'Nati's mom, Nati has her face like this, come pick her up,' or 'What happened?' Something! But no, they just ignored her. Then I found out several teachers saw her like that because they said she was like that since the morning! And nobody called me. Several teachers saw her like that, and nobody said anything. No me le pusieron atención. So with all of that, I can say I am allowed to complain, and say that the teachers were wrong. That they didn't take care of my daughter. They were irresponsible and they put her health at risk. But in the end, nothing happened to the school, and the only thing that happened was that the teacher stopped talking to me. That was it.

"Well, Nati was a long time with her little face like that, almost a month. They had to give her shots. It was all shots and more shots—not pills, just shots. The shots were so that her little face would straighten back up. She had to wear a patch over her eye all day and even at night when she slept because her eye stayed open. The doctor said that if she didn't cover it with a patch, that the air would dry it out. So she had to cover it, and it watered a lot, but it had to stay covered. I made sure to change her little patch every day and night, and I put a little gauze underneath to soak the tears. Every day, several times a day, I had to give her little massages all over her face. I rubbed a little arnica oil on her, and with a warm, warm towel I covered her entire face. Then I would massage her little face with the arnica ointment, y le sobaba y le sobaba. The doctor told me how to massage her face, but she complained that it hurt, so I struggled a lot with her because she didn't want the massages.

"She was very brave, and even though she resisted the shots, she still did them. But it broke my heart because Nati would wake up and look in the mirror. She would look very sad, and with her face still really bad, she would pull at her face. She would pull it up and down and get really angry. She would get angry, and then get very sad, and pull at her mouth, saying that she wanted her mouth like this. It broke my heart. I would just say, 'It's going to go back! You'll see!'

"She had a really hard time eating too. When she chewed, all the food would fall out of her mouth. When her face started getting better, she would point to her mouth like, 'Look, look, it's going!' She would get really excited. I think the arnica helped a lot. When it finally got better, and she could finally move her mouth, I would say, 'Let me see you smile?' And she would move it like this and that, or she would talk. She was very happy when her face got better."

What stood out to me in Claudia's story was the same thing that stood out to her: the school's irresponsibility. Like Claudia, I too felt enraged hearing how an entire school of adults trained to work with children could see a child with such an obvious health emergency and remain silent, act as if nothing was wrong, and not even call her mother to check in. Claudia noted that even her comadre Beatriz would get phone calls from the school if anything was amiss with her daughter. I too had received many calls from the nurse every time my son hurt himself on the playground. My son was just a year older than Nati. In my few interactions with the principal, I knew her to be a serious leader, so I wasn't surprised that she was horrified when she heard what happened, and I wouldn't be surprised if the teacher was reprimanded given her response to Claudia.

But the reality is that nothing was really resolved. The doctor refused to validate Claudia's concern that the major trauma to Nati's ear had caused the paralysis, and Claudia was left with a resentful teacher. The hardest part for Claudia was that only Nati knew what really happened, and was happening, to her at school, and Claudia couldn't be there at all times to keep her safe. These were compounded traumas, and Claudia could only get so far in her advocacy. It was like fighting with the audiologists all over again. An undocumented mother fighting for her undocumented daughter, and no one was *really* listening. I was reminded of a friend who had recently left Texas after years of fighting with school boards to uphold their commitments to students with disabilities in public schools. My friend has a PhD and many years of experience in public advocacy work, and she speaks fluent English. She couldn't get people to *really* listen either. Texas schools have been notoriously failing children with disabilities, and undocumented immigrant children, given their additional barriers, are some of the most affected.[3] Was Nati neglected by the school because of an absolute lack of attention, training, and advocacy for disabled students, or was it because she and her mother were undocumented, or because Claudia only spoke Spanish and the teacher couldn't be bothered with the language barrier? It was very likely all of the above.

"The teachers are always quick to call you when your kid does something wrong, right? They should be like that when something happens to your kid too. One time the teacher called me that Nati had stuck out her middle finger at her. I told her, 'No, she would never do that.' Well, nobody in our house, not even her cousins, do that. And I'm asking myself, 'Well where did she get that from?' So then the teacher called again, that she did it again and that the school wouldn't let it pass a second time, and that's why they were calling. When Nati got home, I told her I was going to chop off her finger if she ever stuck it out again, and since then, bien portadita, she never stuck it out again. Now she behaves. When I ask her if she's behaving, she pretends to be a little soldier. She makes fun, but I tell her, 'Ándale, and if I even hear that you are not staying still in line, I'm going to chop off your finger.' She won't even show me how she did it."

Claudia laughed recounting how she put the fear of God in Nati for disrespecting the teacher. I just nodded and laughed with her. I would've lost my finger too if I ever did that to a teacher, I thought. My dad used to tell me that my hand would dry up and fall off if I ever raised a hand to my parents or grandparents—that if I ever even pretended to make any sign of disrespect, stuck up a finger, slapped at the air, my hand would fall off. I believed it. I knew there were certain lines that should never be crossed. I could tell from Claudia's story that Nati understood that invisible line of respect too. So while the daughter in me connected to Nati's fear of having her finger chopped off for being disrespectful, the mother in me also wondered, with Claudia, what may have provoked Nati to act like that in the first place. Why would a five-year-old suddenly flip off her teacher when she had never done anything like that before? Where did she get that from? What was Nati responding to? Was she frustrated? Was she being ignored again? Did something happen that the teacher didn't acknowledge, and Nati felt compelled to flip the teacher off out of anger?

Claudia told me that Nati was often bullied at school, sometimes even by kids that were supposed to be her friends. They made fun of her hearing impairment, mimicked her way of speaking, and sometimes even physically hurt her. I thought about how I would respond if I were Nati and the teachers, the people who were supposed to protect me, didn't do anything. I might be inclined to flip one of them off too if that's all I felt I had the power to do. Of course, not all kids would respond to injustice that way, but Nati was different. Before she got to the story about Nati's facial paralysis, Claudia had been telling me about Nati's personality.

"She's very complicated, very," Claudia started. "She's not the type of person that likes 'girl things.' Ella es más ruda. I don't know who she takes after. I tell my husband that she has my sister's nature. Nati knows how to defend herself. She's independent. She likes Batman and the Hulk. Those are her favorite characters. Everything she likes you would think is more for boys. If I try to dress her in dresses or little pink things, she won't let me. She hates dresses. I say, 'Mami, but you look so beautiful in this dress,' but no. I don't know, she's strange. And if I do put her in a dress, then she will put on a baseball cap. She carries baseball caps with her everywhere and wears them backwards. If I try to take it off, she pushes my hand away. In all of our pictures she's like that, and she makes this rock and roll sign with her hands. And I ask her, 'Mami, what is that? Where did you learn that?' But yes, that's how she is all the time. She won't wear dresses or skirts, just jeans and tennis shoes. She's like that, and if I say, 'Look! Look at this! Do you like this?,' right away she makes a face.

"Nati is so complicated with her eating too. 'Mami, what do you want to eat?' I ask. She will close her eyes and think. 'A hamburger.' 'No, not that,' I say. 'A hot dog.' 'Not that either,' I say. Other than that, the only thing I can get her to eat is quesadillas. She can eat quesadillas every day. That's okay but she can't just eat quesadillas all the time! But I tell her, 'Mami, you are from Mexico! You were raised on beans!' But I can't even get her to eat beans now. She used to eat all the beans and sopitas and caldito de olla I made her. That's what she ate. I tell her that I have pictures of her covered in beans and sopita when she was a baby.

"Oh, and she loves the dirt—the dirt, bugs, caracolitos. These bugs that in Mexico we call puerquitos. They curl into little balls. She loves them. She isn't afraid of anything. No bugs or animals, nothing. But at the same time, she's super sensitive. One time she was playing with this little bug, and I got scared and told her to throw it away. I shook it off her, and she just started crying and crying. She was so upset, like if a person had died. She was like that when her fish died too. Fíjate, her fish just died yesterday, and she was just crying and crying. The other day also, they were watching a movie and all of a sudden she got very emotional. So the movie was about a dog, I think, but then someone ran over the dog, and she just started crying and crying.

"Her sister was sitting there watching the movie, and Nati got up and stood next to the television and started explaining to her sister everything that was happening in the movie. She would stare at the TV, and then she would turn to her sister and keep explaining, in signs. I was so surprised because her sister is only three, and she doesn't really know sign language, but they were communicating. I wanted to record them, but I don't know, I forgot. I was so focused on them. It was just very strange to see her there, interpreting a movie for her sister. But that's how she is. Es muy atenta, and that's how much the movie affected her. She observes everything that's happening around her, and she records it in her mind, I think. One of her teachers, a long time ago, told me that she has an incredible memory, that Nati will explain things that happened a long time ago exactly, in detail. Sometimes the teacher has to tell her to pay attention to the class, because she will be there observing everything and everyone around her. She tells me everything that her teacher does and everything that happens at school, in detail. If she saw a spider, she will say, 'The spider walked this way.' And the teacher tells me that Nati also tells her everything that happens at home. I ask the teacher, 'Well, what does she say?' And the teacher says that Nati tells her how every night she wrestles in the living room with her sister and her dad. She loves lucha libre, so she and her dad wrestle here on the carpet when he gets home from work. That's what she likes. For her, she prefers playing things that are rougher like that.

"She is very social and loves to make friends. But mostly she prefers the boys to the girls. She has some girlfriends, but she prefers to play with boys. Last year there was this little boy. I think his name was Jason. I don't remember, but she told me that she told him that she was his wife. 'Válgame, Dios,' I said. 'Really?' Because she told me that she told him that she wanted to be his girlfriend—no, his wife—and he said okay, that he would be her husband too. I said, 'Are you serious?' And she said yes. So I told her she better not be going around allowing besitos or anything like that! Then we mess around with her saying, 'Ooh, Nati, you're in love!' I told her I was going to tell her dad, and she puts her hand over my mouth to warn me not to say anything. And like that, we laugh, and I play around and make little heart signs or funny faces at her. But, yes, can you believe that? So she does have many friends, boys and girls. But she also complains a lot to me that the boys push her down or she got hurt playing with them. I guess for her they're playing. That's what she tells me. But there she is, with the boys—it doesn't matter who—playing."

"I thought Vero, Beatriz's daughter, was Nati's best friend. How do they get along?" I asked.

"Well, not really, no. I mean yes, they are friends, but not that good of friends. They play, but they fight a lot too. I really don't understand why they can't get along. Beatriz gets on Vero's case a lot because Vero would make fun of Nati. She would mimic Nati's way of speaking. One day Beatriz told Vero that that's how her brother used to speak, and would she like it if someone made fun of her brother? Of course, she said no, and since then Vero doesn't make fun of Nati anymore. I don't even know how she mimicked her because who knows. They were little, so I know kids don't always know better. But yes, after Beatriz talked with Vero and told her about her brother, she stopped. So they play, and they call each other. They invite each other to play, but it doesn't take long before, boom, they're fighting again and then they're mad at each other again. One day I told Beatriz, I said, 'Beatriz, why do our girls not get along?' Beatriz said, 'Oh, just let them kill each other. Not you and me though. We will always be friends, no matter what they do.' So that's why I say they are friends but not best friends. I think maybe they have different personalities. I don't think Vero is ruda like Nati. Usually when I hear them playing, I hear Vero talk more about girl things, but I don't know.

"You know, I struggle a lot with Nati because she doesn't always tell me what happens with her. If someone does something to her, she doesn't always tell me. So I have to be very attentive. Sometimes she would come home from school with bruises all over her body and bite marks on her back. I would get so scared and say, 'Mami, what happened?' She would say, 'This boy hit me.' Oh, it was bad. She had bruises on her legs and on her bottom. And the teacher would never tell me anything! One day I got so angry seeing her come home like that and the teacher didn't do anything, so I told her, 'No, Mami, tú chíngatelo.' Yes, that time I did tell her to defend herself. I said, 'If he hits you again, you hit him back! I don't want to see you come home again with bruises on your body!' Well, I probably shouldn't have told her that. Well, yes, I should, but at the same time no, because she's already very tough. And now, amiga, she defends herself!

"What I'm saying is, I needed to tell her to defend herself because I'm not there to protect her, and the teachers are not protecting her, and these kids are taking advantage of her. So I say, 'Defend yourself, Mami!' But I feel that I'm teaching her to be aggressive, and I don't want that either. Because the teacher never, never tells me anything that happens to Nati at school.

"Oh, but one time she did call me because Nati beat up this little girl. She hit her in the stomach. Then there was another little girl with ponytails. I don't remember her name, just that she always wore ponytails. Pues, mija se la sonó a esa también. That time the teacher saw Nati, so she couldn't deny it, right? But she didn't even try to deny it. Nati told me she was mad because the little girl had hit her first. She said she kicked her in the stomach and hit her first, and Nati got mad and that's why she hit her back. And, well, the little girl cried. So I told the teacher, 'I know my daughter was wrong to hit her back, and you saw that, but you didn't see when the little girl hit her first.' Can you believe they wanted to suspend Nati for two days?! I told them, I said, 'Now you need to call that little girl's parents, because you called me and I have been attentive to Nati, and now they need to come and answer for their daughter.' I told them, 'I'm here so that you and everyone can see that I am responsible for my daughter. I am taking care of her, and I need that little girl to apologize to my daughter, then Nati will apologize to her.' So that's what they did, and then I told Nati not to fight anymore.

Well, nothing big happened to Nati that time because I was there al pendiente, watching, taking care of my daughter. But the other parents were not attentive to their kids like I was. "Things are better now that she's not with that teacher anymore. Now they call me all the time if Nati gets hurt. They call and say, 'Nati got hurt and we put some ice on it.' I say, 'Okay, is she crying?' And they say no. But I have to go all the time to put ointment on her wounds at school because she's always making herself bleed on her stomach and back. Remember, I told you she has really dry skin. It is so dry that sometimes it breaks or it itches a lot, and when she scratches, she makes it bleed. But the school calls me now. They call me to tell me, 'Nati has this or that.' That's all I want is for them to call me if something happens.

"I think that Nati has made herself tough. Ella busca la manera de ser entendida. She figures out how to let you know what she wants to say or what she feels about something. Even with me, if I don't understand her, she won't stop until I understand exactly what she's trying to say. If I don't understand, she will grab me by the arm and take me to show me what she's saying. If I still don't know, she will scream in frustration and show me a different way. Then she will make a face like 'Now did you understand?' And that's how she will act until I really understand. She knows if I'm faking it too. She knows, and she won't stop finding a way until I really understand her. She, alone, finds a way so that you understand her. Solita ella se las arregla. I tell you, this is a very sensitive topic for me. The tears just come out because I see how hard she tries to be understood.

"When I help Nati study her sight words, she tries to speak them to me, and I feel so bad. I tell her, 'Mami, sign them to me. Show me the signs that represent these words.' And she tells me no and points at me to read the word for her. Then she will go through and mouth letter by letter. I say, 'Okay, now tell me the next word, but in signs,' and she goes back and does the same thing, and I say, 'No, Mami, tell me the sign.' But then I just leave her alone and let her continue that way. If that's how she wants to do it, then fine, I let her do it that way. We go through all the words, then we start again from the beginning, and I say, 'Okay, now tell me in signs,' and then she will say it in signs. But, yes, it makes me very sad because I see that she really wants to speak, and she tries, but then she sees that we understand her better in sign language, and so she will sign. Then we understand her. Sometimes with the kids at school too, especially when she was younger, she would hit a lot. Pegaba feo. Or she would push them so that they would pay attention to her. Even with us sometimes, but now she's learned not to hit. Now she will tap you with one finger. With one finger, she will tap you to get your attention. She does the same at school. She taps the kids to ask them a question or to say 'Let's play' or 'Do you want to play?' And if they say no, she will go play by herself.

"It took her a long time to learn how to communicate. A long time. And me, I learned with her. I'm learning with her. I had access to these videos that I was studying, and so I learned several words. But I don't really know how to talk with other people like her, who are deaf, because I get nervous that I won't know the right sign or that I will forget a sign that I already learned. The same with English. I'm not good at pronouncing things in English, but I understand Nati's English, and when she says something in English, I know what the word is in Spanish. I know what it means, and I can make the connections. But Nati is faster. So I say, 'Mami, slow down, I don't understand you.' For example, her name, she says 'Natalia' really fast, and I say, 'No, Mami, slower, slower.'

"We have met many other people who are deaf, and she gets very shy too. Very shy. She will hide behind me and say 'no, no' and refuse to come out. I say, 'But, Mami, you have to try.' But she's like that only with people she doesn't know. With people she knows, she gets crazy. She plays and acts goofy and says a bunch of things really fast. Who knows what she says! She had a teacher once that she was very communicative with. That teacher was so patient with her. We really liked her. This teacher she has now is a little bit like that too. She's been able to communicate well with her, and she is teaching her more signs. With her, it's been better, and Nati comes home and teaches me and corrects me when I do it wrong."

Claudia was clearly concerned about how Nati was responding to her everyday struggles. She was worried that Nati had to make herself tough to defend herself against the world, and that she had to constantly fight to be understood. Perhaps Claudia was worried about whether Nati was internalizing traumas, social and emotional, and whether that was making her reactive in a way that could be destructive or unhealthy. I thought about Nati's sudden facial paralysis and recalled Claudia's story about fibromyalgia. Claudia couldn't explain how the fibromyalgia started, and neither could her doctors. But fibromyalgia is also linked to sudden trauma—namely, emotional trauma—and Claudia's symptoms started after her traumatic migration across the border. Similarly, Nati's facial paralysis was very likely the result of a physical trauma to her ear, and Claudia knew that, even if her doctor wouldn't affirm it. In both cases, trauma sent the body into shock, and the body reacted, screaming out in debilitating pain or shutting down in paralysis. Nati was clearly dealing with a lot, but it's not easy to know how children are interpreting or internalizing their experiences. Claudia could sense that Nati was struggling to communicate a lot of things, and she worried that her occasional aggression could be concealing something.

It didn't take much to find medical research on the "behavioral difficulties" of hearing-impaired children. One study looked at the differences between deaf children with hearing parents and those with deaf parents.[4] The researchers found that the latter tended to have more behavioral problems than the former, but they weren't sure why. But Nati wasn't just any "hearing-impaired child." In Claudia's words, nobody knew Nati like she did, and she had a gut feeling about her daughter. Nati wasn't displaying "aggressive" behavior because she was hearing-impaired. Her behavior reflected her language and communication struggle, in part, but it was also a result of the mistreatment at school, her urge to hear, and her inherited fighting spirit.

It was also the border. Whether she knew it or not, and I think she did, the border was in the background of it all. This was all part of Nati's migration story—her borderland identity. Nati was straddling three different cultures and languages, and fighting for her own place in all of it. It took more effort to find research on children like Nati: children with hearing impairments and

hearing parents who were also Mexican, immigrant, and growing up in bilingual homes. One article checked some of these
additional boxes but still didn't quite fit.[5] These researchers, who
primarily interviewed Mexican American mothers, argue that
Hispanic parents hold very different views about disability and
disability education than Anglo parents do. According to these
researchers, Hispanic parents tend to default to the authority of
teachers and medical professionals when it comes to their children's health and educational capabilities, presumably giving less
attention to the child's own agency and self-expression. These
parents also emphasize assimilation into North American culture
as the best way for their children to be successful in overcoming
their "limitations."

As I read the article, I kept thinking, That doesn't sound like
Claudia at all. Of course, there are also many differences between
Mexican American families and undocumented Mexican immigrant families. It was nice to see a study that was giving some
attention to cultural differences and bilingualism in perceptions
about disability and disability education, but where did that leave
families like Nati's, undocumented families that share many of
these struggles but have their own particular set of experiences?

It was clear from Claudia's stories that Nati was incredibly
self-sufficient and had learned to defend herself from bullies
and irresponsible teachers and administrators; in short, Nati
had learned to protect herself, and Claudia was, at least partially,
relieved. Claudia described Nati as ruda, which can mean a lot
of different things. She seemed to use it in the sense of "rough"
or "tough." It also translates as "rude," but I don't think that's
how Claudia meant it. Regardless, *ruda* leans more toward the
negative notion of "rough," as in "rough around the edges"—
more so than the potentially more empowered description of
"tough," as in courageous. According to Claudia, Nati had a
rough demeanor and preferred friendships with boys because
they shared more things in common. It was a personality that
Claudia connected to masculinity, and it clearly confounded her.
She questioned where it may have come from (possibly her sister?), but certainly, it seemed, not from her.

I thought it was interesting that she didn't identify any of herself in Nati's personality. Maybe because Claudia preferred friendships with women, her comadres, or liked dresses and "pink things," unlike Nati. But I heard a lot of similarities in their stories. Claudia walked across a desert—alone. She stood up to a coyote in the middle of the desert—alone. For years Claudia took her daughter to doctor after doctor, trying to get her a hearing implant, refusing to accept no for an answer. Like Nati, Claudia consistently stood up for herself and her family in ways that other people almost never have the courage to do.

When I was in middle school, my mom was called to the principal's office who knows how many times. Every time it was something like "Elizabeth was sent to the principal's office for telling the teacher she wasn't allowed to tell her to shut up." Or "Elizabeth was sent to the principal's office for calling the teacher a 'hypocrite.'" According to my parents, I was always "talking back." On one of those occasions, my mom drove me home and said, "Hija, if you always defend yourself, then I'll never have the chance to defend you." It's funny how some things our parents say to us burn a hole in our memories and stay there forever. Like Claudia, my parents also struggled to understand my "ways." Yo también era ruda—tough, outspoken, and not afraid to defend myself. I didn't have Nati's needs, but I still felt like I had to take care of myself, handle my own problems. My parents were attentive, as Nati's parents were, but in my adolescent mind, I didn't want to bother them, and I didn't think they would understand anyway. I could defend myself.

For Nati, perhaps it was about being heard. She wasn't being heard, in multiple ways, and that was frustrating for her, as it would be for anyone. Kids were seemingly ignoring her, and when they did engage her, they often bullied her. The teachers pretended not to see or didn't care. It doesn't matter why. I think that in Nati's mind, they didn't see her. They didn't hear her, they didn't care about her, and rather than that making her sad, I think it pissed her off. I understood that.

Nati was figuring out how to deal with her world, and she didn't accept her hearing impairment as a limitation. In all of our conversations, Claudia made it clear that Nati wanted to hear. "Busca escuchar," she emphasized. "Nati seeks to hear. She wants to hear." That is why she insisted on speaking her words first rather than signing them. It's also why Claudia fought so hard to get Nati cochlear implants as soon as she arrived in the United States. She fought to help her daughter hear despite doctors telling her that Nati was too young and wouldn't take care of the devices, or that Nati had too many languages and wouldn't develop her sign language. Claudia knew these doctors were misinformed. "They don't know her," she insisted. They hadn't spent hours practicing sight words with Nati and seeing how hard she tried to vocalize. I think this is what made the topic so sensitive for Claudia, what made her cry. She was trying to advocate for her daughter, and she wasn't being heard either.

But given the barriers imposed on her, Nati had to adapt. She had to learn to get people, even her family, to understand exactly what she was saying, what she needed. She fought for this every single day. So maybe she had to flip off a teacher or punch some bully in the stomach. She was un-drowning herself. I could hear my grandmother's words as I listened to Claudia describe her daughter's fight. "No te quedes con nada adentro, hija." Nati wasn't keeping anything inside. She wasn't internalizing people's ableist views of her. Maybe she couldn't tell people what she thought of their treatment, but she certainly could show them. At least this is what I imagined.

In one of our conversations, Claudia revealed with intense faith—but also with what I perceived as resigned sadness—that she knew Nati would have more opportunities in the United States than in Mexico, but that, even then, she understood that she would always face more barriers than other people. "Here she can at least have a little career," Claudia said. "She can be an assistant somewhere. She has some opportunities." I don't know why this particular comment stood out to me. Maybe it was the limitation of Claudia's imagination for Nati's careers? There's nothing wrong with being an assistant, but if you're dreaming up a life for your kids, why not make them the boss? I hadn't thought to ask her at the time, but I thought back to the article on the Mexican American parents of hearing-impaired children and wondered if maybe it revealed something about this. Was it that Claudia couldn't see past the medical/institutional view of

Nati's hearing problems as an "impairment" and "limitation"? Or was it an acute and partially embodied understanding of all the barriers Nati would always face? Barriers that went beyond her hearing and that were more about belonging, especially when it came to Nati's immigration status. Or perhaps Claudia just didn't know all of the possibilities at that moment. Migrating to the United States was a massive leap of courage that had opened up possibilities that had before existed only in Claudia's wildest dreams. Getting herself and her family to the best possible future was her goal, but what that future would look like had yet to be seen. And what about Nati's ruda personality, that fighting spirit we spent hours discussing? Was that a limitation or a strength? Claudia feared it could be both.

I think my parents worried about my limitations back then too. We now know that I had anxiety as a child. I was incredibly sensitive, and that meant my emotions were sometimes intense. It meant I was nervous about uncertainty, so I asked a lot of questions, angrily resisted last-minute changes to schedules or interrupted plans, and really hated inconsistencies in rules. Because of this, I often found myself at odds with teachers and my parents. I was easily overwhelmed by noise and a lot of people, which was basically my home life. We lived with six of my tías, uncles, cousins, and my grandparents. There were always somewhere between ten and fifteen people living in our home. Loud and crowded was our environment. For the most part, I loved it, but the fact that it made me flee to my room sometimes for quiet, or get irritable and act out in frustration, unnerved my parents. I know this now because I've learned more about anxiety as an adult and because my son inherited the same emotional struggle. It shows up differently for him, but many of the triggers are the same. When I was growing up, my dad would pray out loud that I would change for my own good. He worried, as Claudia did about Nati, that I was too sensitive and that I would end up getting hurt or that I would suffer a lot. In his eyes, my sensitivity was unnecessary and a choice. My dad used to say that I could resolve so many of my problems with a smile, but that I made the choice not to. All these memories spun around in my mind as I was listening to Claudia try to explain her daughter.

I think she believed that Nati had limitations that would give her only a few options in life, meaning she would have to be tough and fight harder than others even to have those limited options. But at the same time, Claudia didn't want Nati to be so tough. She seemed to regret that Nati wasn't more "girly" and "soft," or interested in dresses and pink things. Like my father, Claudia wished that Nati would just smile more—at least for the family picture. Meanwhile, Nati was throwing up rocker signs, curling her lip, and punching bullies. My parents saw my emotional sensitivity as a limitation too—a roadblock that, because they didn't understand anxiety, appeared to them as self-imposed and something that would limit my life options. And just as Claudia would wonder about Nati, my mom would ask herself where I got my "personality." She often said I was a lot like her mother, my maternal grandmother, Dolores. Ruda like her.

But if I was ruda, it turned out not to be much of a limitation. My traits were exactly the ones I needed to make it through a doctoral program and survive and thrive as a first-generation Chicana scholar and professor. I don't see myself as ruda though. I see myself as confident, determined, courageous—the same way I see Nati, and Claudia, and my mother. But societies have determined these characteristics to be masculine and therefore not appropriate, or admirable, in women and girls. Girls are supposed to be quiet, obedient, and gentle. Like Nati, I wasn't raised by quiet and obedient women. But I wish that girls and women were allowed to express the full spectrum of emotions and to be a whole complexity of personalities, constantly changing, adapting, growing, and always rooted in our environments, without feeling pathological, defective, or somehow limited. Nati had many imposed stereotypes and barriers to face and navigate—the ableism that defined her as impaired, the xenophobia that defined her as "other" and that excluded her from the quality health care she needed, the teachers and school administrators who rendered her invisible, and the gender norms that reduced her fighting spirit to rudeza, roughness, because "that's not how girls should be."

From everything Claudia had told me about Nati, I could see that her fighting spirit was incredibly special. I only imagined

Nati as a boss. In fact, knowing her, there's no way Nati would want to be anyone's assistant. Maybe Nati would grow up to become an artist—perhaps a passionate musician in a rock band. It would be an all-girl band too, because as she grew up, she'd meet other badass women like her in her Feminist Politics course. Or maybe she would major in political science and lead the Undocumented Students Movement at her university. She would be the president, obviously, and her hair would be growing back from when she shaved it that one year in protest of the heteronormative, ableist patriarchy. She would be standing in a classroom, invited by her professor, sharing updates about the movement. She would be so articulate and passionate that the professor wouldn't have anything to add except a signature for the petition she had passed around to support undocumented, disabled students. I have met young women like Nati, and their lives, the boundaries they are destroying, still bring me to tears. Joyful tears of a future that their mothers dreamt up, and that they embody. A future only their eyes can materialize. Nati isn't just a dreamer; she's also a dream come true. But even if Nati doesn't do any of those things, it doesn't matter. It doesn't matter what she grows up to do or be. She will still deserve quality health care and an equitable education, and all the resources she needs to live a healthy life. She will still deserve belonging and safe spaces to un-drown herself, to heal, so that she can live a full life of her own design.

I don't know how Nati's story will unfold. I like to imagine that it will have a happy ending, but I know that life is more complicated than that. The only truth I know is that Nati's story isn't written yet. She's still writing it, and only time will tell what the episodes of her life will look like. Only time will tell which parts of Nati's story will become title-case chapters, which will be forgotten, and which parts will be (re)membered completely anew.

UNDOCUMENTED STORIES

"ON THE NEWS THEY WERE SAYING THAT NOW THEY ARE making a law to separate families at the border. I don't know if you've seen that. Can you imagine if they had caught me with Nati? They would have separated us. Just like that. Ay, no. I can't even imagine it. I've seen that it has happened to so many señoras. They are put in a detention center, and their children are put in another one in another city! How are you going to separate a child like that? I know they are doing that to try to scare people from coming over, but that will never work because people are desperate. Look, independent of anything, how do I explain this? It's like they say, 'Ponen un muro, y pues hacemos un túnel y nos venimos por abajo. De todos modos, nos brincamos ese muro.' In other words, people will never stop coming. No matter what. And I think, what does it hurt them anyway? These people that are coming, they are not coming to ask for money, just asking for money. No, these are people who are buenos para trabajar. They're good workers. Uno trabaja duro. We work hard even though the pay is minimal.

"I've been here five years now. El tiempo vuela, así como si nada. If I could turn back time, far back, to when I was pregnant with Nati. If I had known that Nati would be born like this. In the first instance that my husband came over and everyone told me, 'Leave, leave, leave,' and I said, 'No, no, no,' that I didn't want to leave my family. No sé. No se me antojaba mi vida en los Estados Unidos. I just didn't crave a life over here. But if I had known that Nati would have these problems, I would have left right then, and I wouldn't have thought twice about it. Now that I am here, that I have been here for five years, and they never gave my baby the surgery she needed, I feel like I failed her. I think if I had left sooner maybe, right? Who knows?

"But even with everything we've been through, I would still do it again. If we went back in time, I would still come again because even with everything, Nati has advanced a lot here. She has learned to defend herself! Sola. She has developed solita, on her own. And well, I like the care that she receives here, even with all the problems at school sometimes. In Mexico it's more discriminatory. Right now, my daughter would be playing in the dirt in our home in our pueblo. She wouldn't be in school. School? There? No, there's nothing there for her. We have known people like her who are deaf and who have been deaf from birth like her, but they have no education. They have never been to school because, well, where? The teachers in the regular schools don't understand them and they don't accept them. You would have to move to the city because there it's a pueblito, un ranchito, chiquito. There are no services for her. Entonces, sí, de todos modos, lo haría otra vez. Even in the current conditions, yes, with everything that is happening now at the border, I would do it again. With fear and everything, I would do it again. Y te voy a decir que no cambiaría nada. I wouldn't change anything about my experience porque vivo muy a gusto, and things happen how they happen, right? But the only thing I would change, just one thing, I would make it so that Nati had her surgery and that she could have a little more help for her disability and when it comes to her medical care. I would change it so that she would have access to everything she needs. I wish that she had more opportunities and services for her hearing even though she's not from here. I would change the politics so that she could get more help.

"One time I applied for the Gold Card for Nati, but—remember, I told you—it was just for one year because they would send me to some clinics all the way over there by the West Side. I don't remember what they were called. They also sent me to the LBJ. Everything was in different places and, yes, well, they would take care of her in those clinics, like if she had a cold or a cough or allergies. Because Nati also has allergies and very dry skin. So yes, those clinics would treat her, but it's always for small things like that.

"One time I took her to an ear specialist at LBJ. You won't believe that the doctor there tried to help me get Nati, not like a residency, but like a permission so that she could be here legally. He really didn't focus on her ear but instead on her immigration status. He found us an immigration lawyer. He gave us some signed papers and everything to show that Nati needed assistance and that she needed a residency, a legal residency, so that she could get what she needed. But since she doesn't have papers to be here legally, there was nothing they could do. When they are citizens, they qualify for everything. They can even have the surgery done for free. All of it. So, well, my sister-in-law is in that process of getting her residency, but the people there told us that she couldn't sponsor Nati. Only her sister can sponsor her so that she can have some kind of legal status here. But, well, her sister is a baby so not until she gets older. Otherwise, maybe her uncle could try to sponsor her, but who knows. So when I tell you the only thing I would change is Nati's status, it's because it really makes a difference for her."

"Wouldn't you change your access too?" I asked Claudia, pushing back a knot in my throat, and wondering if even a part of her was thinking about her own health as part of her daughter's needs.

"Primero la niña," Claudia responded without hesitation. "It's like I already told you before. I'm not saying I don't value myself, like I don't matter, but the most important thing to me is my daughters. My daughters will always come first. Mis hijas primero, segundo mis hijas, tercero mis hijas, y al último mis hijas. I just want them to have what they need. As long as they have access to medicine, and consultations, and their treatment, especially Nati, then I'm happy. I worry about Nati the most. When my comadre asked me to leave Nati with her if I ever got deported, I thanked her, from the bottom of my heart, but I said no. I know she cares about Nati very much, but no, I will always stay with my daughter. Es que nadie me la va a ver mejor que yo. I know that no matter how much anyone says they care for her, or they feel sorry for her, they will never care for her like I will. I know there are a lot of people that are ceding their [parental] rights to other people. My sister and brother-in-law are in the process of getting their legal residency too. Maybe, I think, maybe I would pass the rights to them, like for an emergency. In case of an emergency so that they could get her, and so that no one else would take her, and then right away take her to Mexico to be with me. Only like that and only to them. In the case of an emergency that they tried to take Nati away from me, or both my girls, so that my brother-in-law could protect her until I could be with her. But just to give her to someone else, no, never."

Moving back and forth between Claudia's story and her thoughts on Nati, I could see the generational work happening before my eyes, materializing mostly through questions, uncertainties, y mucho pendiente, but happening nonetheless. Despite the border, Claudia was focused intently on being the best mother for Nati—on protecting her future and well-being, but also her life and her heart. Nati, in turn, was focused intently on figuring out how to live her own life. There is nothing exotic about any of that. Mothers don't stop being mothers just because they're undocumented, and mother–daughter relationships will always be complex, regardless of immigration status. But the border was there too, adding an additional layer of life to everything.

Claudia wanted Nati to have the best future, but she wasn't going to sacrifice their maternal relationship for the United States. Claudia's sacrifices had a limit, a line, one that she was very clear she, and nobody else, would ever cross. If they were forced to return to Mexico, they would, together. My dad used to say that everyone must have their own line. "You draw a line, and you live by it," he counseled. It was like a protective barrier, but also a blueprint for making critical decisions for your family. Like Claudia, my mom also drew her line around her children. I thought back to how after sending us away to Mexico, my brother for the second time, she drew her line. She collected her things and left the US to be with us. She hadn't planned to give up her life there to live in Mexico—that wasn't her plan. All she knew was that she wouldn't let a border stand between her and her children any longer; she wouldn't give her children up for a life in the US either. And just as it was for Claudia, this meant making a very difficult decision with a great deal of fear and uncertainty. For Claudia, taking Nati back to Mexico with her if she were deported meant removing her daughter from the life she had worked so hard to build in the US, and therefore potentially exposing her to what she believed was an impossible struggle in Mexico. At the same time, she felt in her heart that Nati needed her mother, and, well, I'm sure Claudia needed her daughter too. I think Claudia knew that no matter what happened, she would figure it out; she would keep fighting for Nati to have the best possible future, no matter where.

Despite the incredible resilience of so many families and mothers, the border robs them of any real choices. Every migrant is following their own line, their heart, with absolute courage, and with faith that they are making the best decision for their families. The line that undocumented parents draw around the protection of their families and, most importantly, their families' futures is powerful and a symbol of love, endurance, and hope. But the line is also carved out of their own bodies—with (im)migrant parents taking blow after blow for their children, every blow weakening their own health, causing irreparable traumas and illnesses they often keep to themselves. Claudia understood that as an undocumented mother, being concerned about the legal protection of her daughters came with the status. Most parents only have to think about their children's patronage in the event that they were to die suddenly. It can happen, but most people don't like to even imagine it, let alone prepare for it. Thinking about or perhaps being tormented by thoughts of who will take care of their children in the event that they are suddenly and unexpectedly deported or, worse, locked away in a detention center is something that all undocumented parents have to deal with.

US immigration policies continue to multiply undocumented mothers and families. More than ever, women and children are the ones facing the treacherous, militarized US-Mexico border.[1] Many of these women and children will become undocumented immigrants, but all are refugees, fleeing violence and economic hardship, and searching for a better life—a future. None of these families have chosen to become undocumented; it wasn't their life plan, and yet this is the situation they find themselves in. As of this writing, thousands of children are being separated from their mothers and caregivers at the border, and mothers are desperately searching for children some haven't seen in years.[2] These children and their mothers are being traumatized beyond repair, and not enough is being done to stop it.[3] There are so many stories like Claudia's and Nati's—stories that have been erased and deflated to a percentage, a "crisis." These untold and undocumented stories, testimonios, of profoundly complex human lives—of courage, hope, fear, prayer, advocacy, failure, success, pain, illness, and healing—have been lost in the noise of xenophobia and the criminalization of migration.

The moment Claudia handed her baby over to a coyote was one of the most painful of her life. The realization that Nati would be separated from her and the fear of not seeing her again took everything out of her and sent her body into long-term shock. As a result, Claudia would live with chronic pain for the rest of her life. I think that was the moment she drew her line. There were layers to Claudia's life that unfolded and revealed parts of her that she didn't always show—parts that were soft and tender and unsettled. There were layers of choice and agency lined with obligation and no alternative. In the folds, illness was reconciled as sacrifice because that's how you keep going, how you keep your children safe. In the folds, comadres rubbed sweet ointment on the tender parts, the parts that hurt, and the parts that just needed compassion. There were layers of migration and transformation lined with the profound wish to stay home, to stay in the womb. In the folds, there was grief and grieving for a life that could have been, a life that wasn't determined by illness and a border. In the folds of every part of Claudia's life was Nati's future driving her to have courage, to get up and get across the freeway, to take herself to the doctor, to keep mothering, even if it was all undocumented.

"Me da mucha tristeza pensar en eso. Me dan ganas de llorar." Claudia spoke softly. "We know we're not from here. We weren't born here, but this is where we built our family, our home, where we struggled to buy the few things we have. When you think about the sweat that it cost you to have this living room, an enormous amount of work to buy these couches that we're sitting on, and then to just have to abandon it all just like that, like it's nothing. It breaks your heart if you think about it. I just pray that if they ever take me, my wish is that they will give me one day to leave. Just one day. I will get my daughters and a few of my things, y feliz me voy. But you know, everything is always calm around here. We don't hear of anybody being taken around here. Aquí todo está muy tranquilo. I haven't been stopped by the police in four years, and there's no reason for them to stop me, right? I'm very careful. I follow the laws. I drive carefully. There's no reason because I don't do anything wrong. Si me llegan a parar, va a ser nomas por que me vieron el nopal en la frente. Nomas por eso. Pero pues hay muchos nopales por aquí. Y así, así llevamos la vida."

AFTERWORD

La Última Rifa

ON OCTOBER 24, 2021, CLAUDIA SENT ME A TEXT MES-
sage to ask if I would participate in one more raffle. Claudia
was raffling off a black leather purse to raise money for Nati's
cochlear implant surgery. She sent me a picture of the purse
and details, but all I could think was, Is this really happening?
"Is it *the* surgery?" I texted back in genuine disbelief. "Yes,"
Claudia responded. "You know how hard we have fought for
this, and now it's finally happening. Solo Dios sabe cuando es el
momento." I congratulated Claudia, the text box woefully insuf-
ficient in translating my joy, and selected my numbers.

The raffle took place that same week over Facebook Live.
Claudia was nervous. "I've never done one of these Lives before,"
she laughed. She was animated and did her best to keep everyone entertained while we waited for people to log on. Nati was
by her side. Once everyone was on, Claudia explained that she
would make the game more interesting by first drawing ten tickets to disqualify. Of course, my name was drawn. The eleventh
ticket would be drawn by Nati, and that person would be the
winner. The suspense was killing me. When it was her turn, Nati
tore into the raffle jar and pulled out the winning ticket.

On November 4, 2021, Nati García got her cochlear implants,
and Beatriz Chávez got a new purse.

ACKNOWLEDGMENTS

I AM THANKFUL TO CLAUDIA GARCÍA FOR INVITING ME into her home and sharing her most intimate memories with me. Being invited into someone's home is a responsibility, and I took that responsibility to heart by treating Claudia's home as I would want mine to be treated, and her story as if it were my own. I appreciate Claudia's vulnerability, her energy, and her sincere willingness to share many parts of her life story with me. Claudia is a natural storyteller. Her emotive and passionate mode of expression not only brought her story to life for me, but also sparked so many questions about my own maternal histories. Muchas gracias, Claudia.

Reflecting on Claudia's life through the multiple layers of her identity and experiences led me to reflect on my mother's layers as well. I am grateful to my mother for her willingness to be a big part of this book. Unlike Claudia, my mother is extremely shy and reserved, and it takes a lot to get her to talk about her experiences and feelings. For all your undocumented mothering, vulnerability, courage, and disposition to open old wounds with me, muchas gracias, Mami. You deserve a book of your own.

I am also thankful to the women who are in this book in spirit because they are the community. I am thankful to Margarita and Beatriz. Their comadrazgo and deep loyalty to Claudia are admirable, and I'm so fortunate to have been able to witness just a small part of it. I found out later that Beatriz encouraged Claudia's decision to be a part of this book. "Ni que tuvieras nada mejor que hacer," she joked. Beatriz also deserves a book of her own, and I am so very grateful I could meet and get to know her throughout this process. Muchas gracias, Beatriz.

My abuelita's spirit is the theory and praxis that speak through this book. I'm grateful for her mothering, her wisdom, and the courage she continues to send me. When my grandmother passed, it felt like a title-case chapter of my life went with her. It took a lot to bring myself back to this project knowing that she wouldn't be here to finish it with me. In the end, it is with her hand on mine that I have been able to finish this book and, with it, open a new chapter and connection to her. Muchas gracias, Abuelita, que en paz descanse hoy y siempre.

The fieldwork leading up to this book was partially supported by the Center for Mexican American Studies at the University of Houston, and the monograph was written with support from a UH Women of Color Coalition Stimulus Research Grant. My graduate student Manuel Rodríguez transcribed some of the last interviews and did so at lightning speed. Muchas gracias, Manuel.

This book may not have come together as it did if not for the early guidance and editorial eye of Elizabeth Bartels (E.B.). For your ability to help me unravel the layers of academic training holding me back from writing the book I wanted to write, muchas gracias, E.B. A special thank-you to my colleagues and friends Dras. Abigail Rosas and Ruth M. López for reading and commenting on an early draft of the manuscript. Muchas gracias, colegas, for your support and thoughtful reflections.

I appreciate Drs. Beatriz Reyes-Foster and Anand Pandian for their incredibly supportive and encouraging peer reviews. Thank you for engaging with the heart and purpose of this book with an eye toward what is possible in anthropology. Publishing my work with the University of Texas Press is always a positive experience, and for that I am truly grateful. For supporting this project years before it was even close, and for his continued appreciation of my approach to anthropology, I am grateful to Edward C. Kittrell. I also appreciate the careful attention and editorial expertise of UT Press manuscript editor Lynne Ferguson and freelance editor Alexis Mills, and the dedication of everyone at the press who helped bring the final book together.

This book was mostly written in the middle of the COVID-19 pandemic, which brought with it a whole host of other emergencies, losses, and traumas. I am grateful to my partner,

Ibraim do Nascimento Santos, for holding down our home with me as we worked together to keep our family safe, guide our son through virtual learning, and care for a very energetic toddler amidst multiple waves of the pandemic. I'm always grateful to my children for keeping me grounded and focused on what matters. They are my greatest teachers. I have learned over and over that anything is possible as long as I am with my family. For all your love, support, smiles, hugs, and protection, muchas gracias, mis amores, Anahita, Oliver, and Ibraim.

NOTES

1. Becoming an Undocumented Mother
1. See, for example, M. Howes, M. Siegel, and F. Brown, "Early Childhood Memories: Accuracy and Affect," *Cognition* 47, no. 2 (May 1993): 95–119.

2. See Rose Marie Perez Foster, "When Immigration is Trauma: Guidelines for the Individual and Family Clinician," *American Journal of Orthopsychiatry* 71, no. 1 (April 2001): 153–170.

See also Obianujunwa Anakwenze and Andrew Rasmussen, "The Impact of Parental Trauma, Parenting Difficulty, and Planned Family Separation on the Behavioral Health of West African Immigrant Children in New York City," *Psychological Trauma: Theory, Research, Practice, and Policy* (January 2021): 1–10.

2. Falsas Esperanzas
1. "Obama's Health Care Speech to Congress," *New York Times*, September 10, 2009.

3. What Sickness?
1. See University of Texas Medical Branch at Galveston, "Hispanic Women Less Likely to Survive Endometrial Uterine Cancer," *Science Daily* (December 2014), www.sciencedaily.com/releases/2014/12/141216100715.htm.

See also "The Crisis of Cervical Cancer among Latinas," *Salud America* (January 2018), https://salud-america.org/crisis-cervical-cancer-among-latinas/.

5. Natalia
1. The Gold Card was renamed the Harris Health Financial Assistance Program (HHFAP) when the system discontinued the use of actual gold cards. County officials found that the cards wrongly encouraged people to think of the program as health insurance, causing considerable confusion. The HHFAP is not insurance and can only be used in the two Harris county hospitals and the Harris Health clinics. Only families that live in Harris County and who meet the income requirements are eligible for the discount program.

2. Lyndon B. Johnson Hospital in Houston is operated by Harris Health.

3. Aliyya Swaby, "Texas Schools Still Failing Special Education Students, Federal Review Finds," *Texas Tribune* (November 2020), https://www.texastribune.org/2020/11/05/texas-schools-failing-special-education-students/?utm_source=articleshare&utm_medium=social.

4. David H. Barker, Alexandra L. Quittner, Nancy E. Fink, Laurie S. Eisenberg, Emily A. Tobey, John K. Niparko, and the CDaCI Investigative Team, "Predicting Behavior Problems in Deaf and Hearing Children: The Influences of Language, Attention, and Parent-Child Communication," *Development and Psychopathology* 21, no. 2 (2009): 373–392.

5. Yessica S. Rodriguez and Thomas E. Allen, "Exploring Hispanic Parents' Beliefs and Attitudes About Deaf Education, *Journal of Latinos and Education* 19, no. 1 (2020): 45–55.

Undocumented Stories

1. See United Nations, "Women and International Migration," *The World Survey on the Role of Women in Development* (2020), https://www.un.org/en/development/desa/population/migration/events/coordination/3/docs/P01_DAW.pdf. See also David Hernández, "Unaccompanied Child Migrants in 'Crisis': New Surge of Cases of Arrested Development," *Harvard Journal of Hispanic Policy* 27 (2015): 11–17. See also Ivón Padilla-Rodríguez, "Child Migrants in Twentieth-Century America," *Oxford Research Encyclopedia of American History* (New York: Oxford University Press, 2020).

2. See, for example, Leandra Hinojosa Hernández, "Feminist Approaches to Border Studies and Gender Violence: Family Separation as Reproductive Injustice," *Women's Studies in Communication* 42, no. 2 (June 2019): 130–134. See also Ivón Padilla-Rodríguez, "The U.S. Separated Families Decades Ago, Too. With 545 Migrant Children Missing Their Parents, That Moment Holds a Key Lesson," *Time* (November 2020).

3. See, for example, William Wan, "What Separation from Parents Does to Children: 'The effect is catastrophic,'" *Washington Post*, June 18, 2018. See also Ragini Tharoor Srinivasan, "The Lasting Trauma of Mothers Separated from Their Nursing Children," *New Yorker* (November 16, 2018).

SELECTED SOURCES

My grandmother liked to say, "Tú tienes tu gente, y yo, la mía. Tu gente no es mi gente, y mi gente no es tu gente, y así es. Y bueno, dime con quién andas, y te diré quién eres." It means you can tell a lot about a person by the people they call community, and you can tell a lot about a writer by the books they engage with. Beyond interviews with Claudia and my mother, and many conversations with family and community, this book also benefited from a community of texts, including ethnographies, memoirs, essays, and scholarly articles that fed my investigation on undocumented health access and my exploration of creative writing in nonfiction and the social sciences. Although not an exhaustive list, here I include some of the texts that were important to this work, and some additional sources that might help guide curious readers into their own investigations and toward their own gente.

Page 4: *"The geopolitical border creates and shapes Mexican families on both sides; it has done so for generations. Even the very sacred notion of motherhood—what motherhood means and how it is embodied and lived by Mexican women—carries the open, throbbing, and fertile wound of the border."* The metaphor of the border as a constructive and destructive element in the lives of Mexican and Mexican American families that underlies and unites the narrative in this book builds on the foundational writings by Chicana feminist and philosopher Gloria Anzaldúa. Using a braided narrative that interweaves lives of mixed-status families, leaves sections of Spanish untranslated, is situated in between genres and disciplinary positions, and is outside of Eurocentric discourses also builds from Anzaldúa's works. See Anzaldúa's *Borderlands/La Frontera: The New Mestiza* (San Francisco: Aunt Lute Books, 1987); see also *Light in the Dark, Luz en lo Oscuro: Rewriting Identity, Spirituality, Reality* (Durham, NC: Duke University Press, 2015).

On Chicana feminisms, see Gabriela F. Arredondo, Aída Hurtado, Norma Klahn, Olga Nájera-Ramírez, and Patricia Zavella, eds., *Chicana Feminisms: A Critical Reader* (Durham, NC: Duke University Press, 2003). See also Cherríe Moraga and Gloria Anzaldúa, eds., *This Bridge Called My Back: Writings by Radical Women of Color* (Albany: SUNY Press, 2015). On the transnational movements of Mexican migrants and the creative ways in which they imagine and reimagine their communal ties across the border, see Alicia Schmidt Camacho's *Migrant Imaginaries: Latino Cultural Politics in the U.S.-Mexico Borderlands* (New York University Press, 2008).

Page 4: *"This book, then, is a tapestry, a weaving together of testimonios, and an intimate witnessing of motherhood between Claudia and me."* The desire to listen in relationship with and in recognition of my own participation in the creation of a story and in the process of storytelling is inspired in part by a wealth of feminist scholarship and anthropology that centers the subjective experience and a relational mode of inquiry and exposition. I especially returned to Ruth Behar's *Translated Woman: Crossing the Border with Esperanza's Story* (Boston: Beacon Press, 1993). I was drawn to the way Behar centered Esperanza's raw narrative in the first two sections of the book, but also reflected on her own positioning as author and her role in framing the story. On the practice of vulnerable writing as a skill that comes with a different set of expectations, I was also inspired by Behar's *The Vulnerable Observer: Anthropology That Breaks Your Heart* (Boston: Beacon Press, 1996).

But one can be vulnerable and still reproduce hierarchies of power. In thinking more specifically about Claudia's illness narrative, and the power dynamics of recording an illness narrative, I took inspiration from Sayantani DasGupta's body of creative work, especially "Listening as Freedom: Narrative, Health, and Social Justice" (in *Health Humanities Reader*, New Brunswick, NJ: Rutgers University Press, 2016). DasGupta develops the concept of *narrative humility*, a type of listening and storytelling that recognizes the limits of our own understanding of any one person's life, and the many complexities, contradictions, and limits of the narrative itself.

The narrative style of this book is also inspired by a long tradition of storytelling, as shared and communal experience, in Mexican communities. Here I use the concept of *testimonio* as a particular form of Latinx storytelling and relational practice, a collective witnessing and communal healing. While there are several critical conversations on *testimonios*, I was especially inspired by the Latina Feminist Group and their edited volume, *Telling to Live: Latina Feminist Testimonios* (Durham, NC: Duke University Press, 2001).

Page 5: *"Living in the United States as an undocumented Mexican immigrant is to live with extreme uncertainty. Claudia's story, although recounted as memories, was saturated by the everyday struggles of the present moment, but also stubbornly focused on the future."* This book was also inspired by memoirs and essays written by (im)migrant writers working out their own identity formations vis-à-vis the border and race politics of the United States and their own hopes and dreams for the future. For example, see Valeria Luiselli's *Tell Me How It Ends: An Essay in Forty Questions* (Minneapolis: Coffee House Press, 2017); Grace Talusan's memoir *The Body Papers* (Brooklyn: Restless Book, 2019); and daughter of immigrants Michelle Kuo's *Reading with Patrick: A Teacher, a Student, and a Life-Changing Friendship* (New York: Random House, 2018). And see Edwidge

Danticat, whose body of work has inspired me since before I even knew I wanted to write this book—especially *Create Dangerously: The Immigrant Artist at Work* (New York: Vintage Books, 2011).

Page 34: "*The idea that immigrants are stealing or wasting public resources is unfounded and, frankly, just cheap xenophobia peddled gratuitously by politicians and the media.*" Health care polices have historically been coupled with immigration policies and restrictions that have left undocumented immigrants and their families locked out of health care based solely on their immigration status. The 1996 welfare and immigration reforms especially exaggerated the rhetoric of the time, claiming that US borders were "out of control" and that immigrants, particularly Mexican immigrants, were depleting public resources. These 1996 policies and reforms came on the waves of violent national debates about immigrants' rights to public education, public health, and other social services, further igniting an overall hostile environment for immigrants. See, for example, Leo Chavez, *The Latino Threat: Constructing Immigrants, Citizens, and the Nation* (Stanford, CA: Stanford University Press, 2008); Jessica M. Mulligan and Heide Castañeda, eds., *Unequal Coverage: The Experience of Health Care Reform in the United States* (New York University Press, 2018); and David E. Hayes-Bautista, *La Nueva California: Latinos in the Golden State* (Berkeley: University of California Press, 2004). On the criminalization and erasure of Latinx immigrant humanity and personhood, see Lisa Cacho, *Social Death: Racialized Rightlessness and the Criminalization of the Unprotected* (New York University Press, 2012).

Page 39: "*I also couldn't help but think of the history of medical experimentation on Mexican and immigrant women and girls conducted by racist scientists during the time of eugenics in the United States—experiments used only to tag and label them as pathological, incompetent, unworthy, not enough, or too much. Medical practices that traumatized an entire population for generations.*" Historically, US health policies have rendered undocumented Mexican women's bodies unworthy of care insomuch as it might represent the possibility of a healthy future. These policies are situated in a history of medical racism and exclusion that have long pathologized the reproductive practices and cultural values of Mexican-origin women. Throughout the twentieth century, Mexican-origin women were often institutionalized and sterilized after being medically classified as "unfit" and biologically unable to control their own fertility, and were often medically described as "morons" and "feebleminded" for their "non-normative" sexuality. Still, medical records documented "disdain" for Mexican women that went beyond their sexuality and that pathologized their cultural practices, religious beliefs, and personal lives. Stories like these are abundant in the literature and not far removed from the contemporary moment. See Natalie Lira and Alexandra Minna Stern, "Mexican Americans and Eugenic Sterilization: Resisting Reproductive Injustice in California, 1920–1950," *Aztlán: A Journal of Chicano Studies* 39, no. 2 (2014): 9–34; see also Elena R. Gutiérrez, *Fertile*

Matters: The Politics of Mexican-Origin Women's Reproduction (Austin: University of Texas Press, 2008).

Page 52: *"We may never know how many undocumented Latinas suffer from fibromyalgia or other stress-induced illnesses—from the strain and complexity of an undocumented life compounded by gendered demands, chronic pain, and the stigma of an invisible illness, screaming but unheard."* For an intimate discussion on the multiple and complex ways in which Latinas experience chronic illness, see, for example, Angie Chabram-Dernersesian and Adela de la Torre, eds., *Speaking from the Body: Latinas on Health and Culture* (Tucson: University of Arizona Press, 2008).

Page 59: *"My mom is not a very religious person, and as a Chicana she had her own sense of mexicanidad. If you asked her, she would never call herself a marianista, or any of the other words that have been used to label 'Latina reproductive behavior' as exotic and pathological."* For an ethnography on how Mexican immigrant women in New York think about and express change, transformation, and agency within their reproductive practices, see Alyshia Galvez, *Patient Citizens, Immigrant Mothers: Mexican Women, Public Prenatal Care, and the Birth Weight Paradox* (New Brunswick, NJ: Rutgers University Press, 2011).

"Comadres" chapter, beginning on page 69: For an additional conversation on the critical female bond of comadrazgo between Latinas, see Lillian Comas-Díaz, "Comadres: The Healing Power of a Female Bond," *Women and Therapy* 36, nos. 1-2 (2013): 62–75. Also see Adela de la Torre, "Countering the Pain that Never Heals," in *Speaking from the Body*, edited by Angie Chabram-Dernersesian and Adela de la Torre (Tucson: University of Arizona Press, 2008), pp. 44–56. De la Torre discusses the idea of *pláticas*, or intimate conversations between comadres, as a form of spiritual and emotional healing that in turn helps relieve stress and heal traumas that can aggravate the physical pain caused by musculoskeletal disorders.

Page 71: *"People participated because it was affordable and because they would need the help one day too. The raffle itself represents lives that are fundamentally grounded in community, where resources are often shared and where families and neighbors engage each other to improve their conditions together."* For a detailed historical and deeply personal account on relational community practices in mixed Mexican immigrant and Black communities, and the ways in which these communities support one another despite histories of systemic oppression, see Abigail Rosas, *South Central Is Home: Race and the Power of Community Investment in Los Angeles* (Stanford, CA: Stanford University Press, 2019).

Page 107: *"Or maybe she would major in political science and lead the Undocumented Students Movement at her university."* On the college experiences of undocumented youths in the United States, see Roberto G. Gonzales, *Lives in Limbo: Undocumented and Coming of Age in America* (Oakland: University of California Press, 2016).

Page 112: *"Moving back and forth between Claudia's story and her thoughts on Nati, I could see the generational work happening before my eyes, materializing mostly through questions, uncertainties, y mucho pendiente, but happening nonetheless."* For an intimate historical account on transnational family life and the creative ways in which Mexican families embrace the spirit of difficult decisions concerning the future of their families, see Ana Elizabeth Rosas, *Abrazando el Espíritu: Bracero Families Confront the US-Mexico Border* (Oakland: University of California Press, 2014). See also Leisy Abrego, *Sacrificing Families: Navigating Laws, Labor, and Love Across Borders* (Stanford, CA: Stanford University Press, 2014).

CPSIA information can be obtained
at www.ICGtesting.com
Printed in the USA
BVHW080754160922
647187BV00017B/350